Ellis Amdur

Words of Power

A Guide for Ordinary People to Calm and De-Escalate Aggressive Individuals

Words of Power: A Guide for Ordinary People to Calm and De-Escalate Aggressive Individuals©

Ellis Amdur, M.A., N.C.C., C.M.H.S.

A Message to My Readers
I am committed to sharing the best of my years of experience and study with you. Please respect these intentions by adhering strictly to the copyright protection notice you'll find below. Thank you for your vigilance in respecting my rights.

Notice of Rights

Limited Liability and Disclaimer

Credits
Cover Photograph: Jessie Eastland – Own work, CC BY-SA 4.0,
    https://commons.wikimedia.org/w/index.php?curid=44276721
Design: Soundview Design

Published Works by Ellis Amdur

Books on De-escalation

NOTE: These books are each expanded, profession-specific versions of the work that you have in hand, for those who must deal with aggressive and emotionally disturbed individuals on a regular basis.

COOLING THE FLAMES: Communication, Control, and De-escalation of Mentally Ill & Aggressive Patients – *A Comprehensive Guidebook for Emergency Medical Services,* By Ellis Amdur & John K. Murphy www.edgeworkbooks.com

EVERYTHING ON THE LINE: Calming and De-escalation of Aggressive and Mentally Ill Individuals on the Phone *A Comprehensive Guidebook for Emergency Dispatch (9-1-1) Centers,* Ellis Amdur www.edgeworkbooks.com

FROM CHAOS TO COMPLIANCE: Communication, Control, and De-escalation of Mentally Ill, Emotionally Disturbed and Aggressive Offenders *A Comprehensive Guidebook for Parole and Probation Officers,* By Ellis Amdur & Alan Pelton www.edgeworkbooks.com

GUARDING THE GATES: Calming, Control and De-escalation of Mentally Ill, Emotionally Disturbed and Aggressive Individuals *A Comprehensive Guidebook for Security Guards,* By Ellis Amdur & William Cooper www.edgeworkbooks.com

GRACE UNDER FIRE: Skills to Calm and De-escalate Aggressive and Mentally Ill Individuals in Outpatient Settings: 2nd Edition *A Comprehensive Guidebook for Health and Social Services Agencies, and Individual Practitioners,* Ellis Amdur www.edgeworkbooks.com

IN THE EYE OF THE HURRICANE: Skills to Calm and De-escalate Aggressive and Mentally Ill Family Members: 2nd Edition, Ellis Amdur www.edgeworkbooks.com

SAFE BEHIND BARS: Communication, Control, and De-escalation of Mentally Ill and Aggressive Inmates *A Comprehensive Guidebook for Correctional Officers in Jail Settings,* By Ellis Amdur, Michael Blake & Chris De Villeneuve www.edgeworkbooks.com

SAFE HAVEN: Skills to Calm and De-escalate Aggressive and Mentally Ill Individuals: 2nd Edition *A Comprehensive Guidebook for Personnel Working in Hospital and Residential Settings,* Ellis Amdur www.edgeworkbooks.com

SAFETY AT WORK: Skills to Calm and De-escalate Aggressive and Mentally Ill Individuals *A Comprehensive Guidebook for Corporate Security Managers, Human Resources Staff, Loss Prevention Specialists, Executive Protection, and others involved in Threat Management Professions,* By Ellis Amdur & William Cooper www.edgeworkbooks.com

THE THIN BLUE LIFELINE: Verbal De-escalation of Mentally Ill and Emotionally Disturbed People *A Comprehensive Guidebook for Law Enforcement Officers,* By Ellis Amdur & John Hutchings www.edgeworkbooks.com

Other Books on Psychology and Tactical Communication

BODY AND SOUL: Toward a Radical Intersubjectivity in Psychotherapy, By Ellis Amdur (Amazon CreateSpace)

SHAPESHIFTING FOR LAW ENFORCEMENT CNT/HNT: Effective Scenario Training for Crisis/Hostage Negotiation Teams, By Ellis Amdur and Sergeant (Ret.) Lisbeth Eddy www.edgeworkbooks.com

SHAPESHIFTING FOR CORRECTIONAL FACILITY CNT/HNT: Effective Scenario Training for Crisis/Hostage Negotiation Teams, by Ellis Amdur and Sergeant (Ret.) Lisbeth Eddy www.edgeworkbooks.com

THE COORDINATOR: Managing High-Risk High-Consequence Social Interactions in an Unfamiliar Environment, By Ellis Amdur and Robert Hubal www.edgeworkbooks.com

Fiction

THE GIRL WITH THE FACE OF THE MOON, By Ellis Amdur www.edgeworkbooks.com

CIMARRONIN: A SAMURAI IN NEW SPAIN By Neal Stephenson, Charles Mann, Ellis Amdur, and Mark Teppo, Jet City Comics (Amazon Publishing)

Classical Martial Arts

DUELING WITH O-SENSEI: Grappling with the Myth of the Warrior Sage http://www.freelanceacademypress.com/

HIDDEN IN PLAIN SIGHT: Tracing the Roots of Ueshiba Morihei's Power http://www.freelanceacademypress.com/

OLD SCHOOL: Essays on Japanese Martial Traditions http://www.freelanceacademypress.com/

Contents

Acknowledgments

My thanks to a wonderful cadre of critical readers, who assisted me in honing this book so that it fits the needs of ordinary people who, very occasionally, must deal with aggression. They pointed out that too much information concerning aggression could be overwhelming rather than helpful, particularly if that information is not directly relevant to their lives. With their aid, I've carved away at a large boulder to offer something that can fit in anyone's hands.

In gratitude to Cynthia Spada, Magali Messac, and Aliyah Asghar. Thanks, also, to my fierce editor, James Dietrich.

Introduction

Why does anger disturb us so much? Of course, some of us may have experienced real violence, a horrible but thankfully relatively rare event in modern societies, but the far more common experiences of being shouted at, cursed, or enmeshed in an argument can also be incredibly upsetting.

To understand why even angry words make us fearful for our safety, we must go back in time. Humanity developed in a very dangerous world, and we have retained a brain that is still primed to perceive it that way. We humans spent most of our evolutionary history in small bands of probably no more than fifty, and often far less than that. We maintained loosely held territories, followed game and gathered foodstuffs, invariably meeting other bands, who had different gods, and different customs. As much as we humans sometimes delight in novelty, we also fear what is strange because, unknown, it is unpredictable. Throughout human history, our response to those who are different has often been violent. In fact, our 'pre-history' is a chain of uncountable mini-genocides: one tribe destroying, or at best, defeating and absorbing another.

Until modern times, each tribe saw themselves as the only humans in a world of beings fundamentally different from themselves; they were surrounded by a world of 'others.' In other words, there were only thirty, forty, sixty people in the entire world. What happened in our own community was all we knew. Others were not only irrelevant to us; for the most part, they were unheard of, unknown. The only exception was occasional meetings to trade goods, or more frequently, raids and wars. We only cared about what happened to 'humans'—the members of our tribe. What that meant is that if one of our tribe were killed, it was a devastating loss. For example, in a band that had ten adult men, one man dying was the loss of a tenth of the entire male population, who were essential as hunters and often as warriors. Even if we, the other members of the tribe, didn't like him, his loss was incalculable. Our brains are still wired to see the world in the same way, even thought the world and society around us is vastly different. We respond to news of violence, of tragedy or the like, however far away it might be, as something that happened right next door, to someone with whom we have had a life-long connection.

With the advent of civilization and our explosive trajectory upwards into this modern world, our knowledge of others is now worldwide. We tap online and read an article about a woman in Pakistan, blamed for her own rape by the elders of her village and forced to marry her rapist; of blood-diamond wars in Sierra Leone; harassment and violence against gay men in Chechnya; of pensions promised, yet unpaid in Greece; of a mass school shooting in Parkland, Florida, or Newtown, Connecticut. In all of these cases and infinitely more, the victims are a world away, yet our brains respond as if they are right next-door. On the one hand, this is wonderful; we are all becoming one human family, and our empathic connection to others spans the globe. On the other hand, given that media defaults to writing about tragedy and atrocity, the world seems to be a hellish place.

With such background noise, is it any wonder that when we are confronted by someone who is verbally aggressive or threatening, our brains are primed to expect the worst? When our daily news is filled with stories of terrible things that we are helpless to stop, part of us, at least, believes we are also helpless to stop what is right in front of us. A cross word may seem to bear the potential of injury or even death. Even though almost all aggressive interchanges are not violent, each still takes a small piece out of us, particularly when we do not know what to say or do. When the angry customer or family member slams her hands down on the front desk, yells and then kicks the door open on her way out, you may have been unhurt. But if you sat there not knowing what to do or say, you experience yourself to be a victim, with the sense that the only reason you are physically unhurt was due to your assailant's choice, not yours.

This book, therefore, is for people who may occasionally potentially interact with emotionally unstable or hostile individuals: in other words, it is for all of us. It is not a physical self-defense book: truly, such books can be a useful supplement to actual training, but if you really wish to learn to physically protect yourself against violence, you must be taught, in person, by someone expert in self-defense and furthermore, expert and trustworthy as a teacher.

This book is also not a 'specialty' book for people whose profession or circumstances require them to regularly interact with potentially violence or emotionally disturbed individuals. As you can see on the introductory pages listing my published works, I have written a number of books specific to the needs of police, mental health professionals, security officers and a variety of other professions. These books go into much greater depth in a number of areas than need to be covered here—because these individuals have a professional responsibility to stay (or in the case of families who live with a mentally ill loved one, must stay) in circumstances that we should escape.

This work is a guidebook for ordinary people who, while simply living their lives, occasionally encounter aggressive people. They can be customers or fellow employees, strangers on the street or elsewhere, or even family members.

A primary focus of this book will be the recognition of potential aggression, and the verbal de-escalation of such unstable individuals before violent acts occur. You will become skilled in assessing if someone is truly dangerous. In many situations, you will have the ability to calm them as well. You will then embody a trait that can be termed 'grace under fire,' that ability to become the center of gravity within a crisis situation so that it coalesces into an ordered system around you. In a surprising number of situations, aggressors will become willing to comply with directives, even anxious to meet your approval or gain your respect.

Let us refer back to points I raised earlier in this section: when you have a sense of power and control, when you know how to recognize potentially aggressive individuals and how to respond to their verbal violence and aggressive behaviors, that 'background noise' that the media creates, rumors of wars and troubles far and near, will no longer have as much influence upon you. When we do not feel powerless in our personal life, the things we hear about people far away will evoke pity and compassion, but not fear and helplessness. When one feels more powerful, one can greet life in all its aspects with a sense of spacious confidence.

Sometimes You Need to Escape, Not De-escalate: Why This Book is NOT The Answer For People in Domestic Violence/Intimate Partner Abuse Situations

I must underscore that this is NOT a handbook on how to de-escalate a perpetrator of domestic or partner violence. In that kind of situation, you are essentially a prisoner of a terrorist: you cannot make things better with better communication strategies, guiding that man or woman to treat you with kindness and respect. The solution is to escape. I urge anyone in such a situation, be you male or female, young or old, to contact a local organization that supports victims of abuse and intimate violence—in many cases, your best avenue is to start with the police.

SECTION I

What Can We Do
To Make Aggressive
Situations Less Likely?

CHAPTER 1

Above All Things,
Be Polite

This phrase may seem like an odd way to start a book concerning potential violence. Yet some of the most powerful people you may ever meet are among the most polite. Courtesy is the ability to behave so that we do not needlessly engender conflict or fear, and most gracefully lead others to more peaceful behavior. When you feel so in control of a situation that you have time to be polite, you can *afford* to be polite. This spacious sense that you have all the time in the world to handle a problem is communicated to the other person—you manifest strength without being threatening. And this establishes a powerful calm in many circumstances.

The purpose of this book is to support ordinary people in Western societies to live peacefully and safely, with a minimum of conflict. It is focused specifically on interactions with people who are aggressive, even on the edge of violence. In short, I focus on that window of time where we start to get scared.

Figure 1   An Example of Powerful Courtesy

A waitress was working a table with a difficult customer. He was demanding, critical and rude. It was obvious that he was simply looking for something to get mad at. He was the kind of guy who enjoyed pushing the other person past their limits and when they lost *their* temper, he used this as justification for his own actions. He was raising his voice to her and waved an arm, when he inadvertently brushed his fine wool coat off of the back of his chair and onto the floor.

The waitress held up her hand and, interrupting his tirade, said in a strong quiet voice, "Sir, you dropped your coat. Let me get it for you." Keeping her hand up as a kind of barrier, she stepped backwards, held calm eye contact, squatted down and picked up the coat. She arose, and carefully brushed it off. Then, maintaining a calm demeanor, she stepped forward and handed it to him. The fight went out of him—all he could do was thank her.

It was not that she was nice to him. Had she merely bent over and tried to retrieve the coat, he would have taken it as his due, because she was *supposed* to serve him and take his abuse. However, by stepping back, maintaining eye contact throughout, and embodying both strength and dignity, she somehow communicated two things at once—she could protect herself (as she was demonstrating), but she also refused to be 'part' of his fight, unless she had to be. This paradox—powerful courtesy—short-circuited his aggression.

CHAPTER 2

The Development Of
A Safety Mindset

It's All About Attitude!

No matter who you are, there is always a possibility that you may find yourself in the midst of an unpleasant human interaction. This is not to say that you must go through your day in a state of hyper-vigilance, constantly on guard against an attack. Instead, you must develop a relaxed general awareness of your surroundings while always being prepared to protect yourself and others. Although I could make this dramatic, using terms like 'the mind of the warrior,' this would only serve to put the concept out of reach. Rather, consider two parents, in the middle of a conversation, ready but relaxed, as their toddlers climbs up the ladder on a jungle gym. Another example would be driving down a highway at high-speed, listening to music, conversing with a passenger, *and* drinking a cup of coffee; nonetheless, you are ready for a car suddenly braking up ahead, or a distracted driver swerving into your lane. If we live our lives the way we drive, or the way we watch over our children, we will have naturally aligned ourselves with the principles in this book. For one final image, think of a cat walking on a fence: graceful, ready for anything, not focused on anything in particular. (And if you can't see yourself as a cat, I'm not talking about physical grace. You can drive your motorized wheelchair; you can maneuver your cane or walker through a subway turn-style, or get up from the cushions of an over-stuffed couch like a cat. <u>It's attitude, not athletic skill I'm talking about here!</u>)

Aggression Doesn't Occur In A Vacuum

Many aggressive incidents develop due to our lack of attention to fundamental safety precautions. They rarely occur without some recognizable precursors. An unfocused mind will impair your ability to notice these early warning signs. Conscious action, taking potential danger into account, is one of the best safety strategies a person can manifest. Consider how you walk when you are aware that the pavement is slippery. You step firmly, look for handholds, and try to keep your knees relaxed, so that you can adapt your posture if you begin to slide. This is no different from how we should interact with strangers, with co-workers or even family members. Regarding the latter, given our fractious political discourse in both America and Europe, can you manage your interactions with family members who hold different political views and still have a good time at the next family gathering? When you are successful, notice how you anticipate when the conversation is getting heated, and how you change the subject, deflect things with humor, even concede a point that is not worth arguing. This is the same type of proactive awareness that we can bring to potentially hostile and dangerous situations.

Finally, such mindful action is not a once-and-done event. It is something you must attend to each and every day, just as you need to check your mirror every time you change lanes.

Reviewing Past Aggressive Encounters

Take some time to reflect on the aggressive and/or violent incidents that have occurred in your life. Think back and try to reconstruct the patterns of behavior that might have preceded the other person's aggression, as well as any actions on your part that were either unhelpful or contributory towards the individual becoming angry. Recall the following:

- What were the circumstances that led to the aggressive encounter?
- What was the *first* sign that indicated that the situation was getting volatile or dangerous?

- What did the individual say in the moments just before the aggressive incident?
- People are generally able to control their verbal expressions better than their non-verbal signals, so remember the individual's body language prior to the incident. Emotional upset can also create a change in the quality of the voice such as rate of speech, pitch, and/or volume.
- Consider what your thoughts were at that time. We very frequently have some advanced warning of an assault, such as a stray thought that we mistakenly discount as being unfounded. Did you minimize, contextualize, or otherwise resist looking at the situation head-on?
- Consider what you felt, physically and emotionally, at each stage of the encounter. The sensations evoked within the context of an encounter with another person are physical expressions of intuition. <u>When you next experience that same sensation be aware that it is an early warning sign that a similar situation may be developing.</u>
- What do you believe you should have done differently? Can you think of something *else* that you could have done (or could do now) to head-off or short-circuit the aggressive incident as it was developing?
- What planning did you do in regard to that individual subsequent to the aggression? How did that plan work?

Figure 2   I should have known . . . In fact, I did

Gavin de Becker, in his great book, **The Gift of Fear**, notes that fear is such an uncomfortable emotion (<u>It is supposed to be uncomfortable</u>!) that we often have a tendency to avoid the *fear itself* rather than the reason we are afraid. Some people talk themselves up ("I'm being silly"); others criticize themselves ("I'm being judgmental," or "I'm being prejudiced") to talk themselves out of the genuine perception that someone nearby is dangerous. Your basic maxim should be, "If I am afraid, there is a GOOD reason for me to be afraid. Where/what/who is it?"

SECTION II

Recognition Of
Patterns Of Aggression

CHAPTER 3

The Cycle Of Aggression

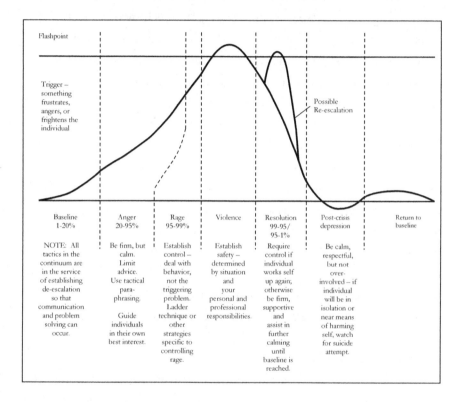

Flashpoint

Trigger – something frustrates, angers, or frightens the individual

Possible Re-escalation

Baseline 1-20%	Anger 20-95%	Rage 95-99%	Violence	Resolution 99-95/ 95-1%	Post-crisis depression	Return to baseline
NOTE: All tactics in the continuum are in the service of establishing de-escalation so that communication and problem solving can occur.	Be firm, but calm. Limit advice. Use tactical para-phrasing. Guide individuals in their own best interest.	Establish control – deal with behavior, not the triggering problem. Ladder technique or other strategies specific to controlling rage.	Establish safety – determined by situation and your personal and professional responsibilities.	Require control if individual works self up again; otherwise be firm, supportive and assist in further calming until baseline is reached.	Be calm, respectful, but not over-involved – if individual will be in isolation or near means of harming self, watch for suicide attempt.	

An outburst of aggression occurs in a cycle that starts with relative calm and ends with relative calm. The aggressive cycle often appears to start with an apparent *triggering event*, though, in fact, the crisis may have been fulminating for some time. The reader may recognize the term 'trigger,' being familiar with it in terms of relapse in regard to substance abuse. Just as many addicts have certain triggers that elicit the urge to use drugs, aggressive individuals have triggers that **cue** them to become violent.

Figure 3.1 Are we helpless against our triggers?

Although an aggressor may claim, even believe, that when they are triggered, that they are helpless to fight their aggressive impulses, this is simply not true. Were it so, we would have no moral agency whatsoever. Being 'triggered' is how one's feels—it is not an objective reality. Instead, when one is 'triggered,' one feels unchained from moral and social rules—the person *lets go* of constraints and the dogs of hell are unleashed.

Baseline: From 0-20

When we are calm, we are at *baseline,* which is represented as "0-20" on the accompanying chart. At baseline, we use the parts of the brain most responsible for our better human characteristics: thinking, creativity, and forming social relationships. The reason that the rating scale goes up to "20" is that I wish to underscore that one can have a fairly intense level of heat and energy, and still be fully rational. For example, one can debate politics with someone with radically different views, and refrain from insults or attacks on the other person's character.

Anger: From 20-95

A triggering event elicits a change in both thinking and feeling. This event can be something that threatens the individual's sense of safety; frustration at not being able to obtain what they desired; or simply a cue that they are now justified using a skill (aggression) with which they are confident. At early stages, the individual first becomes irritable, then angry.

If baseline is represented as being "0-20" on the scale of aggression, with actual violence being "100," irritation developing to anger is denoted by the numbers 20 through 95. These are not numbers representing frequency: rather, they represent levels of intensity. Regardless of the numeric value, angry people are, by definition, still trying to communicate with you. Rather, communicate *TO* you. Their focus is what they have to say—angry people have a limited interest—or none at all—in what you have to say. That's why you hear such phrases as:

- "Just listen to me a second!"
- "You don't get it!"
- "I'll spell it out slow enough for you to understand!"
- "How many times do I have to repeat myself?"

Because we perceive the angry person's attempts to communicate to be obnoxious, domineering, frightening, or just plain irrational, we often do not construe their actions as communication. The angry person, on the other hand, experiences an increasing sense of frustration, desperation, and eventually, a sense of helplessness at their inability to make themselves understood. This further fuels their anger. There are several reasons people get angrier as the perceived or actual conflict continues:

- Some people simply cannot accept anyone disagreeing with them, especially when they believe they are right.
- When you do not seem to grasp what they are saying, they perceive you as being disinterested, or too stupid to understand. In other cases, your lack of comprehension implicitly accuses *them* of stupidity or unreasonableness.
- When you do not agree or comply with an individual, you are frustrating them in achieving something they desire.
- Many individuals have a hypersensitive sense of 'respect.' Resistance, disagreement, or perceived slights are experienced as being disrespectful towards the individual, causing them to lash out in anger or violence in an effort to regain their credibility. This hypersensitivity could be called 'brittle self-esteem;' any challenge to his or her own self-image is experienced as an attack or mortal wound. It is particularly common among abusive individuals in relationships, and in those who have adopted the values of any criminal sub-culture.

As an individual becomes more agitated, the areas of their brain that express basic emotions take over. Rather than adding 'color' to our thoughts, their emotions now run everything. At this point, equity, negotiation, or compromise becomes less and less attractive. In their frustration, angry individuals shift, increasingly, to attempting to dominate you, to *make* you see things their way.

Think of arguments that **you** have had when you became angry. You spiral upwards, becoming progressively more intense, often raising your voice (as if that will help the other person understand) because you want to get through the barriers that the other people is apparently putting up (so it seems to you) keeping you from being understood. Despite our intentions, this type of escalation is counter-productive, because we tend to make less sense when we are angry.

Anger is accompanied by physical arousal, which functions as a feedback loop, driving us toward further arousal. When our heart beats 10%-15% above baseline due to emotional excitement, we no longer care about the truth. We care only about being 'right' and proving the others 'wrong.' The disagreement has become a win-or-lose situation. We interrupt more frequently, cutting other people off, and we only listen to them to pick out the flaws in their argument.

To de-escalate and control an angry individual, you should attempt to *'line up'* with them (something that will be discussed in detail throughout this book). This does not mean you agree with them; you are simply demonstrating that the message got through. When you line up with the individual, you prove that you understand what he or she is saying, thereby proving that his/her concerns are important to you. This in itself is powerfully disarming, not only calming them down, but also helping you to work together to actually solve the problem. This is not as simplistic as it sounds. When you line up with someone, you remove the pretext for anger. You have not agreed with them, true, but you have established that they succeeded in their communication.

Rage: From 95-99

Rage is represented as 95-99 on the aggression scale. These numbers symbolically indicate that there is a very small, often very quick transitional period between anger and violence. How can you tell the difference between anger and rage? When someone is angry, you may respond by becoming angry too. You might also become concerned, upset, hurt, confused, or frustrated. Usually, however, you are not afraid. Why? Although angry people may *later* become violent if they are further agitated, that is not their aim. Instead, their intention is to communicate with you, albeit dramatically, loudly or forcefully. At worst, they are trying to dominate or intimidate you into doing what they want. As unpleasant as this may be, it is still communication.

When individuals are enraged, however, they are, in effect, trying to 'switch themselves on' to become violent. Many people slowly work themselves into a state of rage as a prelude to violence. Others may lash out violently with seemingly no prior warning, verbal or otherwise. However, even non-communicative individuals will usually signal their anger or intentions through their body language and other non-verbal forms of communication.

Even rage does not result in violence most of the time. One reason for this is that we have various self-inhibitors that work to control behaviors and prevent us from acting out our baser instincts. Within a state of rage, an individual is *trying* to overcome those inhibiters, so that they can do what they actually desire—violence. Below are some of the primary internal inhibitors:

    1. **A fear of consequences.** The fear of counterattack, legal repercussions, social disapproval, financial costs, and a host of other possible negative outcomes serve to inhibit one's resorting to

violence to settle a dispute. In other words, if I put 'A' together with 'B,' I'm not going to like the result.

2. **Morality.** Most individuals possess a core set of moral principles (some religious, some not) that hold them back from harming others.

3. **Self-image.** A man may see himself, for example, as the kind of person who does not hit women, make a public display of aggression, or lose control of himself. Another person may see herself as caring, nurturing, and empathetic to the plight of the less fortunate. Fears of tarnishing a positive self-image will often dissuade an individual from committing a violent act.

4. **The relationship.** A feeling of responsibility toward the other person—for example, friendship, love, and family relations—will hold some people back from violence.

5. **Learned helplessness.** Some individuals, survivors of abuse for example, have tried to defend themselves in the past and have repeatedly failed. They may believe that fighting back is a futile effort, only leading to further pain and abuse. Their rage, however, is there: inside. Consider phrases like, 'a cornered rat,' or 'the worm turns,' that describe a person who has suppressed their rage, sometimes for years, before acting out in violence.

Rage, therefore, is a set of behaviors, including both physical actions and verbalizations that serve to do away with one's self-inhibitors, so that nothing holds the person back from violence. Individuals in a rage state are no longer trying to communicate; they are working themselves up to an attack.

Anger is like a rocket ship, all fueled up, with some fumes coming out, and the countdown initiated. Rage is right before lift-off. The rocket has not yet moved, but there are flames and steam billowing out, a terrible roar so loud the ground shakes. It is a roiling moment of explosive, tenuous equilibrium. Fuel could still be cut to the rocket engines so that it sits silent on the launching pad, but there are only a few seconds to act, because the rocket is about to lift off. Lift-off is the equivalent of the initiation of *violence*.

<u>What you *should* experience in the presence of an enraged person is fear</u>. This is not a bad thing. Fear tells us that we are in danger and that we must do something: NOW! Fear switches us on, so that our internal emergency response systems are activated. Fear demands attention, but it should not paralyze us into mental or physical inaction. A sense of powerlessness is not a given when one experiences fear; rather, it is a *conclusion* that some people reach when they are afraid, limiting their ability to control the situation, or to defend themselves.

To deal with the enraged person, you must establish **control**, not only of the aggressor, but of yourself as well. Control tactics, whether they are verbal or physical, are geared to establish the conditions that make the enraged individual no longer dangerous.

Figure 3.2 The Difference Between Anger and Rage

Imagine someone hands you a huge plastic container. Through its translucent sides, you can see a dark, hairy shape, a Goliath Bird-Eater, the world's biggest spider. It rustles around the container which shifts in your hands like its filled with mercury. Is it creepy? Sure it is. Is there any reason to be afraid? Not really. As long as the lid is firmly on the container, you are absolutely safe. This is the equivalent of anger. Internally you say, "I'd better keep the lid on this thing."

Now, imagine your 'friend' takes the container back, and to your surprise and horror, takes off the lid. The spider emerges onto the floor right next to your leg. It raises its front legs in threat-display and exposes its one inch fangs. There is something poisonous, hairy, and mean in the room, and it is not enclosed in any container! The spider is out of the box. This, metaphorically, is rage.

However, the fear that now arises within you doesn't mean that you are helpless. You can step on the spider or jump up on a table. If you are ticked off enough, you can grab your 'friend' by the neck and make him sit on it! A belief that you are helpless near the spider is an interpretation, not a fact. Fear is simply the warning cry—the drums at the brink of battle—that demands that you *must* act right now.

To deal with the enraged person, you must establish *control,* especially if their behavior presents an immediate threat to you, to themselves, or to others. Control tactics—be they verbal or physical—are geared to establish the conditions that make the aggressive person no longer dangerous. In essence, using my metaphor above, we say, "Put the spider back in the box. Now!"

Violence: 100 On The Scale

Violence does not begin when someone is hit or injured. Violence also includes someone making you afraid of imminent danger and attack. Some of the legal terms for this are terroristic threats, harassment, stalking, assault and menacing. In short, a violent act occurs whenever there is good reason to believe that you (or someone else) are about to be hurt. In the face of such a situation, your guiding principle is to establish **safety**, and you must use effective means of protecting yourself and those around you. Very often, the best thing to do is to escape and get help. In other occasions, you hide. In still other occasions, you fight back.

Although actual physical self-defense tactics are well beyond the scope of this book, they are necessary if you wish to develop your abilities to be safe in as many circumstances as you can. If so, you should avail yourself of any defensive tactics and self-defense training that is available. As with any skill, self-defense techniques must be practiced regularly to ensure their viability in the event of an actual confrontation.

Figure 3.3 The Question of Self-Defense

It is possible that some of my readers are very interested in the subject of verbal de-escalation and control, but the subject of self-defense, either unarmed or with weapons (including firearms), may make them very uncomfortable. For many women in particular, the idea of practicing to maim someone or carry a firearm, however justified and necessary the act may be, is utterly alien. Paradoxically, training in effective methods of self-defense enhances one's ability in verbal de-escalation and control. First of all, violence, rather than an ominous threat 'over the horizon,' becomes something with which we are familiar. It is still frightening, as it should be, but no longer a terrible unknown. Secondly, if we have no confidence in our ability to protect ourselves, when we face an aggressive person and try to deal with them, we cannot help but worry, "What if this makes him madder?" or "What if I say the wrong thing." This lack of confidence steals power from our words, and we are *less* likely to be effective. When we have an answer to the 'what if' questions, we simply speak with more authority and confidence, whether or not we change what we say.

CHAPTER 4

Why Would An Individual Become Aggressive?

Aggression is not an alien or unnatural emotion. Without a capacity for aggression, humanity would never have survived. Yet, much aggression is irrational, self-destructive, vicious, and/or cruel. Why would someone be swept by rage when it causes so much harm? Why would people be prepared to throw away their future, even their lives, driven by emotions that they themselves might be horrified to have expressed even a few moments later? <u>You can better control an aggressive individual when you understand what has driven them to anger or rage.</u>

Anger and rage can develop because the individual is **confused or disorganized**. They cannot understand what is going on around them or 'inside' them, due to cognitive distortions or a chaotic situation (too much information for them to figure out). Among those who experience this confusion are those who are mentally ill, autistic, developmentally disabled, intoxicated, and those experiencing overwhelming emotions.

Some individuals feel **helpless, enclosed, trapped**, or beset with a myriad of seemingly unsolvable problems. This is often similar in effect to confusion or disorganization, but it is accompanied by a particular anguish. The individual usually perceives one person or one entity as the cause of their situation, and they fight desperately to get free from their influence or oppression. If you pressure or intimidate a person, be it physically, emotionally or psychologically, you should expect this response.

The fear of attack elicited by an **actual or perceived invasion of personal space** is often a precursor to aggression. Each of us has a sense of personal space, a 'bubble' within which an outsider is only permitted if invited (Chapter 33). In stressful or volatile situations, you will be perceived as an attacker if you encroach upon another's personal space, no matter what your intentions.

An individual may resort to aggression if they **feel they are being wronged, or feel as if they are losing power**. This is especially true of paranoid individuals who may believe that they are being oppressed by systems or powers beyond their control. Depending on circumstances or your profession, they may designate you as the representative of the controlling entity.

Hallucinations and delusions can also play a significant role in the likelihood of aggression with some mentally ill or substance-abusing individuals. The individual may feel compelled to act as his or her hallucinated voices demand. Others become agitated or violent as they try to make the hallucinations stop by any means. On other occasions, the voices, visions, smells, or sensations are simply distracting and irritating.

Anything that elicits profound emotion can cause an individual to become volatile or aggressive. **Emotional stressors** can include a recent loss through the death of someone close, dysfunctional family dynamics, romantic and other interpersonal relationships, job loss or threat of same, sanctions, divorce, infidelity, or feelings of insecurity.

The use of **drugs and alcohol** can certainly make an individual more likely to become aggressive. Addicted individuals can become desperate in the throes of their addiction. Others use drugs or alcohol to let loose impulses they would otherwise control. As I have said to victims of domestic violence regarding their substance-abusing partner: "He doesn't have an alcohol problem. He has an alcohol answer. Whenever he feels like hitting you, he has a few drinks to make it possible."

Organic stressors such as a lack of sleep, a lack of regular exercise, and/ or an insufficient or non-nutritious diet also increase the likelihood that someone will be aggressive. Such deprivations can cause changes in perception, mood, and cognition, which can lead to irritability or hypersensitivity.

Families often function as emotional traps; there is no escape from the people who, although loved, cause us the most pain. This doesn't only pertain to your family—domestic violence often is carried to the workplace.

People in **romantic relationships** often demand that the other person submit to their wishes. There are numerous pretexts to fight, from money to sex to childcare to infidelity, but the rage is fueled by the same source: "You will 'love' me on my terms."

For some, aggression, like its mirror-twin, suicide, is a 'problem-solving' activity or a 'what the hell' response when **one has already given up.** Related to this is a person's belief that he/she has no effect on the world. Violence ensures that you will make an impact. Depressed people, particularly males, often manifest this type of aggression.

Some people would not engage in aggression unless they had been **set-up by others**. They are provoked by family members or friends who use the aggressor as an instrument of their vicarious desire to inflict harm. For example, a man's wife says to him, "I cannot believe you let your boss treat you like that. I thought you were a man, but I see I married a spineless little boy." Other people do this to *themselves* by 'fronting,' making a scene in front of others (friends, family, or coworkers) to increase their status in their 'pack.' Then, out in front, they are afraid to back down.

One of the most powerful driving forces of aggression is **a sense that one has been shamed or humiliated**. Shame is not a mild sense of social embarrassment; it is a sense of being exposed and victimized by others, with no hope of relief. Shame and humiliation are driving forces for revenge-based aggression. Some people brood about past grievances, their anger slowly escalating until they explode into rage or violence.

Individuals may act aggressively out of a sense of **protective rage**, expressed by an individual who is trying to protect another individual whom they perceive as being victimized. The closer one is to the perceived victim, the more aggressive the person will be in their defense.

Some individuals resort to aggression due to a sense of **entitlement.** They believe that if they desire something, they are entitled to it, and will use any means necessary to obtain that which they desire.

Others simply take **pleasure** in intimidating others and acting violently. For them, there is a joy in making others submit and a delight in causing pain.

Figure 4   Why is 'Why' Important?

How can you use the information in this chapter? Aggression and violence often seem to occur instantaneously—how is a person's motivation even relevant? Consider, however, that much inter-personal aggression occurs between familiars: co-workers, customers, family members, friends or neighbors. If you am aware that a person has lost his job, is using drugs, has been storing up grievances—any one of the criteria listed above—you will be more than usually mindful while interacting with that person.

This doesn't mean that we must hide from such people or cease interacting with them. Consider holding a spoon as opposed to a knife; you are more careful handling the latter implement, yet as dangerous as a knife can be, you probably use it in cooking or other chores on a daily basis.

Imagine you've just been informed that the knife in your hands was smeared with a poison: if you get scratched, you will die. You will now handle the knife very carefully, and 'interact' with it in a limited, circumscribed way—putting it carefully away, and warning family members not to touch it. However, if you take proper care, you will be as safe as you would be handling a spoon. It would be far more dangerous if you didn't know the 'why.' Just as I would like to know that the knife is poisoned, I would like to know—BEFORE HE ARRIVES—that my cousin, who is coming over to the house to pick up his gardening tools, just broke up with his wife, is being investigated by Child Protective Services and has been binging on methamphetamine for a week

CHAPTER 5

What Does Escalation Look Like?

As an individual escalates their aggressive behavior(s), they are priming their bodies to posture, to intimidate, to fight, or to flee. They can display a variety of different behaviors:

- **Nervous, anxious, or frightened demeanor.** Such individuals usually lash out in defense. They are not looking for a fight; they are trying to protect themselves.
- **Overwhelmed or disorganized behavior.** Individuals speaking in repetitive loops, pacing and muttering incoherently to themselves, are displaying symptoms of a chaotic mental state. Unpredictable, they may react to you with sudden, unexpected aggression.
- **Hostility.** Any individual displaying open expressions of dislike or hatred should obviously put you on guard.
- **Seduction.** Seduction is not reserved for just sexual expressions or desires. Seduction is any attempt by someone to make you collude with them: for example, "C'mon. It's not even addictive. You aren't going to report me stress relief? No, it makes me work better. You mean to tell me you never got high?" The danger here is that if the seduction fails, the person becomes enraged that you will not play along.
- **Mood swings.** These involve rapid shifts in mood and emotional affect, from boisterous to morose, then shifting to belligerence. Such individuals present a particular risk due to their unpredictability and their inability to control their own emotions.

- **Hypersensitivity.** Hypersensitive individuals—at the extreme end, those with a paranoid character (Chapter 21)—can react aggressively to even the most harmless attempt at communication. They always perceive you as having hidden, ulterior motives towards them.
- **Authority complex.** When you try to set limits or say 'no,' these individuals become frustrated or outraged, refusing to comply with rules.
- **Electric tension.** This is the feeling you get before a thunderstorm hits. I cannot underscore highly enough that you must ALWAYS trust this feeling, this intuitive sense that you are approaching a dangerous situation (Chapter 32).

Changes In Cognition (Thinking Patterns)

As an individual escalates, they prime their bodies, posturing in threatening or dramatic ways. Their thinking patterns also change:

- **Interpersonal cognitive distortions.** Cognitive distortions are patterns of thought where the individual makes broad, negative assumptions. For example, a man is running late for a social engagement and assumes his girlfriend will break up with him. Although he will be a mere five minutes late, he becomes depressed that their relationship is over before he even arrives. Interpersonal cognitive distortions occur when the individual infers the worst of what *you* are saying. For example, you say: "Tia, you have to stop cursing. You run the risk of one of the other employees making an official complaint. I don't want to see you get in trouble." And her response is, "WHAT? YOU ARE GOING TO TRY TO GET ME FIRED???!!!!!"
- **Becoming less amenable to reconciliation or negotiation.** The person focuses on dominating the situation rather than trying to find a peaceful resolution. They may even be correct in what they say, but their focus is on being 'right' in order to win the argument.

- **Deterioration of concentration and memory.** This causes difficulty in the individual's ability to communicate, or to solve problems.
- **Deterioration of judgment.** Their judgment consequently becomes worse and worse. Angry, they cannot evaluate what is really in their own self-interest.

Changes In Patterns Of Verbal Interactions

You should be aware of changes in verbal interaction with angry people:

- **Silence.** Potentially aggressive individuals may lapse into a morose, sullen silence, often accompanied by signs of physical/emotional tension such as hunched shoulders, knitted brows, and glaring at the floor or at other people.
- **Sarcasm.** Sarcasm can be considered to be hostility shaded by passive-aggressive phrases.
- **Deliberate provocation.** Angry people will do or say things to deliberately upset or irritate you. Provocation is a challenge, an attempt to elicit a response that they then use to justify themselves in becoming increasingly hostile.
- **Playing word games.** Some angry individuals will deliberately twist or misinterpret what you say trying to confuse you, or make you question your own memories of previous incidents.
- **Abusive or obscene language**. The use of abusive or obscene language should put you on guard immediately, <u>particularly</u> if the language is threatening or directly demeaning. In this case, the individual uses language to shock or stun you, so that you end up focusing on the horrible things they are saying, and not on what they are doing: such as moving ever closer, or surreptitiously reaching for a weapon. (This is different from the kind of obscenity that is merely an uncouth embellishment of speech, where there is no hostile intention in what they are saying, i.e., "I went to the f*ckin store to buy some damn beer, because I was f*ckin thirsty!")

- **Repeated demands or complaints.** By making constant demands, the individual is looking for a pretext to legitimize their sense of grievance, creating an issue they consider to be worth fighting about.
- **Clipped or pressured speech.** Some individuals couch their aggression by appearing to be overly polite. They often use very formal or stilted language, presenting themselves as being in control when they are actually seething with aggression or a sense of injustice. This is often the hallmark speech of someone with paranoid traits (Chapter 21).
- **Implicit or abstract threats**. As with threatening sarcastic remarks, any implied threats made by an individual must never be ignored. These are individuals who boast of past acts of violence, or who warns people that they might not be able to stop from reacting the same way in the future. "If I ever lost my temper with you, I don't know what I'd do. I hope that never happens."

Changes In Physical Organization

The following are possible changes in physical organization that an angry individual may exhibit as they escalate into aggression. This doesn't mean that all of these facial expressions or physical postures are guarantees of assault—rather, they are behaviors *associated* with aggression, whether it is physically expressed or not:

- **Facial expressions.** The following list is not hard-and-fast, but there is a real possibility of heightened aggression when the person displays:
    a. **Clenched teeth.** This is an attempt to contain or control intense emotions.
    b. **Bared teeth.** This is a threat display. You may have noticed certain people smiling who are really baring their teeth. The eyes remain wide open, as opposed to a genuine smile, where the smile fully involves the muscles around the eyes.

c. **Hooding of the eyebrows and lowering of the chin.** These are automatic behaviors in anticipation of a physical confrontation.

d. **Frowning.** This is often associated with anger.

e. **Staring eyes.** Staring eyes can be an attempt at intimidation or manipulation; targeting the other as prey, particularly if there is tension in the cheeks and all around the eyes

f. **Biting or compressing the lips.** These manifestations are associated with barely controllable intense emotions.

g. **Quivering lips.** This is associated with fear or unhappiness.

h. **Tightening the lips.** This is associated with an attempt to control or contain intense emotion.

i. **Pulsating veins in the neck.** This is associated with building anger and rage.

j. **Dilated pupils in the eyes.** This is associated with drug intoxication.

k. **Avoiding all eye contact.** This, <u>when coupled with other expressions of aggression</u>, is associated with planning an attack, hiding intentions of an attack, or, paradoxically, an attempt to disengage so that they will not be forced to fight. Remember, without those other signs, a person avoiding your eyes, can be shy, intimidated or socially uncomfortable.

- **Breathing**. Potentially aggressive people can display several different breathing patterns:

a. **Shallow, rapid, and irregular breathing pattern.** Frightened people, who may exhibit defensive-aggression, usually breathe in a shallow, rapid, and irregular pattern, almost like panting or gasping. Some hyperventilate, and they may become violent out of a terror-induced panic.

b. **Deep breathing pattern.** Individuals, who intend or even want the confrontation, often breathe very deeply, from the abdomen through the chest.

    c. Smooth easy breathing pattern. 'Professionals' at violence often maintain a smooth easy breathing pattern throughout.

Changes in Actions

- As an individual becomes increasingly **tense and agitated**, they may try to discharge the tension by pacing, often typified by rapid jerky movements.
- **Deliberate rejection in word and deed.** They actively reject any attempt to calm the situation down.
- **Posturing.** They begin to posture, inflating their chests and spreading their arms to make themselves look bigger, invading their victim's personal space, pacing, smacking their fist in their hand, breathing faster, etc. They may move in quick jerky starts and stops, moving toward their victim and then back again repeatedly, as if working themselves up to attack. These actions are an effort to intimidate, prior to adopting a fighting pose.
- **Positioning.** Individuals looking for a <u>fight or confrontation</u> square off directly in front of their target, while those looking for a <u>victim</u> tend to move to the corner of the person, trying to obtain an advantageous angle on them so that they can attack more easily.
- **Fighting pose.** A combative stance, as opposed to posturing, is often a crouch, with the chin tucked in and the hands raised. In some instances the individual may brandish a fist or a weapon. Be aware, however, that those most skilled at violence can often attack from a position of complete relaxation. Such predatory individuals (Chapter 16), tend to *relax* when they are preparing for an attack. They are at home with violence, like a tiger or a snake. These individuals sometimes smile while making eye contact with you.
- **Trespassing and power testing.** An aggressive individual may violate your personal space, getting too close and then backing away, either to establish dominance or test your response, even

'accidentally' bumping into you. The individual may also test their victim's willingness to defend themselves by picking up, mishandling, or even breaking their possessions.

- **Visual sexual assault.** Males, in particular, will use their eyes to trespass on women, *deliberately* running their gaze over their bodies in a kind of 'visual rape.'

- **Displacement activities.** Individuals may hit, kick, or throw objects in an effort to discharge tension, as a threat display, or as a 'warm up' to an attack.

- **Making a dramatic scene.** The individual acts loud, upset, hysterical, either to get closer to you than you would let someone who was clearly menacing you, or to get you so fixated on calming them down so you lose sight of the larger issue of your own safety.

The Edge Of Attack

An aggressive individual is on the edge of attack when the following are exhibited:

- **Skin Tone.** ANGRY individuals have a <u>flushed</u> face: the pale skinned turn red, and the dark skinned turn even darker. In essence, blood at the surface of the skin is a threat display, as if to say, "See how angry I am!" ENRAGED people <u>blanch</u>—light skinned people turn bone-white, and dark skinned people get a grayish, ashen tone. <u>The threat is now</u>.

- **Pacing, muttering, kicking, etc.** Increased pacing, while muttering, brings one closer to the edge or attack. Some individuals engage in more and more displacement activity: hitting, kicking, and throwing things.

- **Internalizing all signs of assault**. Others will *internalize* all signs of incipient assault, and thus, when it occurs, it seems to appear instantaneously. Right before the attack, however, these people often stop breathing a moment, accompanied by the sense of a 'calm before the storm,' as if you are not there. The individual will have a 'thousand-yard stare,' where they seem to look beyond or through you. Some individuals, particularly, but not exclusively psychotic aggressors, get an eerie smile on their face, one that holds no mirth.

- **Acting Berserk.** As the attack is incipient, the individual can *'lose it,'* shaking, yelling, and acting berserk.

Explosion

Violent assault can be either verbal (accompanied by threats or mock attacks) or physical. At this point, you must do whatever you must do to ensure your own safety and that of those around you, up to and including the use of force to control the individual and the situation.

Figure 5 Homework

This may seem like an overwhelming amount of data. Remember, above all else, what I offered earlier: if you are frightened, there's a good reason to be, even if you don't know why. . . yet. You can easily train yourself to use the information in this chapter, however. Make a copy of the criteria (and perhaps that in Chapter 4), and when you see aggressive people in film clips on the news, or in television shows or movies, name what you observe. See if you can pick up early signs in building aggression in a character in a movie. For example, the bad guy smiles, but his eyes remain open and staring—he's baring his teeth, not smiling at all. You have all the information you need, right through your television set.

SECTION III

De-escalation Of Angry Individuals

CHAPTER 6

Preemptive De-escalation

Sometimes an angry individual comes into your worksite or to your home—a little heated, but still rational. Perhaps their baby woke up while you were hammering shingles on the roof of your house, or they ordered something in your restaurant and are really surprised at how small the portions are, even though it is standard for your 'small plate' establishment. They are upset.

Sometimes, however, all they need is some **clarification or the solution to a straightforward problem**. Ask what they want or need. If you have a solution to the problem, explain it clearly to them, give them an idea how long it will take and what they should do in the interim. Always try to explain the process. With the proper information, they de-escalate on their own. This is particularly valid with both service-level or neighborhood complaints, where the person is irritated, rather than extremely angry. For example:

- "I'm sorry that you found our menu unclear, and it wasn't apparent that our portions are small. Tell you what, how about if we add desert on the house."
- "Anne, I'm really sorry. I've got to get these shingles up before the bad weather hits. Otherwise, the house is going to be flooded. I expect it will take about two more hours. I know, I'm sorry. The little guy needs to sleep. Look, let me make it up to you. I'm going to be carting these old shingles to the dump. If you've got anything you have to get rid off, I can take it in the same load. And these shingles are supposed to be good for

fifty years. It'll be the last time you'll ever have to hear me hammering away up here."

When someone with whom you are familiar comes in clearly out of sorts, **introduce your concern by stating impartially that you believe something is upsetting them**, and that they do not appear to be themselves today. Do not pose your concern as a question, such as "What's wrong with you today?" or "Why do you seem so upset? Is there some sort of a problem?" By asking a question, you give the individual an opportunity to simply deny that there is a problem, or take offense that you are 'getting in their business.' Instead, use phrases like:

- "You are really down today. Something is going on."
- "You looked really stressed out when your son dropped you off this morning."

These phrases give the individual an opening to present their problem to you while leaving the power in their hands to choose how they want to respond.

If the individual chooses to respond to you and begins to discuss the issue, use **open ended questions** regarding possible solutions that require them to respond, such as:

- "I get that you are upset, but how do you think you should take care of it?"
- "What do you think can be done to fix this?"

Open-ended questions are intended to keep the power in the other person's hands by encouraging them to consider their options. If they begin to engage in a dialogue with you, this can give you an opportunity to suggest other potential solutions to their problem, or to discuss the possible ramifications of the individual's suggestions, without it seeming like you are 'taking over.'

Please note, however, that questions, even 'open-ended questions,' should only be addressed to an individual who is <u>mildly upset</u>, not to one who is truly angry or enraged. The questions are used to 'slow down' the individual, to make them think. An enraged individual is beyond processing your questions, let alone being ready to think about alternative solutions. Likewise, if you notice that your questions are making the individual angrier, <u>stop asking</u> because questions 'demand' answers, and an angry or enraged individual will view your continued questioning as an interrogation or a failure to understand their problem.

Sometimes, the situation can be resolved simply by **allowing the individual to tell their story**. There is no need to problem-solve and no need to interrupt. In such cases, listening with attention and respect is all that is needed.

Figure 6

If you have ever cared for a small child, you are familiar with pre-emptive de-escalation. For example, I've recently been helping out with the care of my nineteen month old grandchild:

- He gets cranky when he's hungry, and it happens really fast. We never go anywhere far without snacks.
- He has gotten obsessed with certain TV shows that have cars. His parents limit his television watching (Good parents!). A blank screen is fine, but if he sees the remote control, he gets very upset (and he can't yet speak, so it becomes a tantrum). We hide the remote control, unless it is time for the *adults* to turn on the TV.
- When his parents leave, they know to be very matter-of-fact, say "goodbye," and <u>leave</u>. He cries for thirty seconds and then he's done. Were they to linger until he wasn't upset at all, they'd be in the doorway forever.

Similarly, we sometimes know the soon-to-be-upset person well enough that we know what to say and do to head off their anger. We should also know that the earlier we intervene ("You looked really ticked off after your mom's phone call"), the easier the intervention. The longer you wait or try to avoid the issue, the angrier the other person will become.

CHAPTER 7

Physical Organization
In The Face Of Aggression

How you stand, how you breathe, how you use eye contact, and gestures are all essential factors in calming aggressive individuals. You can say all the right things, but if you look like you are afraid, irritated, or angry, your verbal interventions and commands will have little to no effect, and the situation will only get worse.

How To Organize Your Body

The following information will help you organize your body when dealing with aggressive individuals:

- **Move smoothly.** Agitated individuals startle easily, and any sudden movements or gestures on your part may be interpreted as an attack. By moving smoothly, you not only try to keep the person calm, but you also hope that the individual begins to mirror you: if you are calm, maybe there is no crisis after all, and they calm down as well.

- **Breathing.** When you are centered, people tend to feel calmer in your presence. Think of people whom you know who, when they walk in to volatile situations, everyone calms down. Think, also, of people who flame things up the moment they appear. Were you to track their respective breathing patterns, you would probably be able to predict what was going to happen simply by observing two or three breaths. Circular breathing (Chapter 36) is one of the most important skills you can master.

- **Eye Contact.** In most cases, try and establish some type of eye contact. As with the other aspects of body language discussed above, you must be both non-threatening and non-threatened. Glaring at the individual with hostility or darting your gaze around nervously will just serve to make the individual more ill at ease or angry, and may actually cause them to attack pre-emptively. Eye contact, however, is NOT staring the person down—**it is a gaze, not a glare**:
  - It is unlikely that most of my readers here will have many encounters with individuals in psychotic states (see my profession-specific book if this is to be expected as part of the job you do). But it can happen to anyone: you visit a friend and their adult child has stopped taking his or her medication, or you are approached on the street by someone clearly in the throes of psychosis, whether due to a mental illness or drug use. Many psychotic individuals find eye contact to be very invasive. Particularly when they are calm, or only slightly agitated, angle your body in such a way so that they do not feel confronted or forced to make eye contact with you. Even with these individuals, however, you must make eye contact to establish control if they escalate into real aggression (at that time, their aggression supersedes whatever mental illness they may be suffering from).
  - Some individuals may be so frightening that you feel apprehensive about making eye contact with them. Others are so chaotic or manipulative that you find yourself unsure what to do or say when your eyes meet. Look BETWEEN their eyes, at the center of their forehead. You will find yourself far calmer, and the other individual will not be able to tell that you are **looking at their skin rather than in their eyes**. You will just appear very powerful.
  - Regardless of the exact nature of the situation or the individual's mental state, **never look totally away from the ag-**

gressive individual. An attack takes but a split second, especially in close quarters, despite your body positioning and spacing. The individual must be aware that *you* are aware.

- **Stand at an Angle.** You stand with one foot in front of the other, the back foot at a 45-degree angle with some space between them, thus angling your body. Do not line your feet up, heel to heel ("L-Stance"). There should be a space of at least as wide as one or two fists between where your heels fall on the 'east-west' axis. Of course, this stance also allows you to react more easily to an attack. (See the photographs right below on page 45 in the bullet point, "Using your hands as a calming fence").

- **Sit at an Angle.** You should also sit with an 'angled stance' in many situations. You sit on the edge of your chair, with your lead foot flat on the floor, and your other placed on the ball of the foot. You look interested and attentive, but in fact, you can easily get up without the use of your hands or needing to lean forward to get back on your feet.

- **Spacing—how you affect the space between you and another person.** Are you too close to the person? Do not forget that people also have a sense of personal space, and some individuals may regard any intrusion into their 'zone' as an attack (Chapter 33). Particularly if you are a 'close talker' by nature, step back so that the individual does not feel pressured or intimidated.

- **Spacing—how the other person affects the space between you and another person**. Is the individual too close to you? If an individual keeps trespassing into your personal space, tell them calmly that you are happy to talk about their situation, but they should step back, because they are standing too close. You should not display any signs of fear or unease. By responding calmly and firmly, you are letting the individual know that you are alert and aware of danger, as well as able to take care of yourself.

- **Quiet Hands.** When communicating with an aggressive individual, minimize hand gestures and other movements that could be misinterpreted as an attack. When adopting a comfortable stance, clasp one wrist with the other hand. Do not clasp one hand in the other because, if you are nervous, you may begin wringing them unconsciously. This will make you look scared and perhaps evoke the aggression you are trying to avoid. By clasping your wrist, you broaden yourself slightly, and you will feel solid rather than nervous. Furthermore, you can easily bring your hands upward to fend off or block a strike, without looking like you are preparing to do so. There is no apparent fight in your stance, just strength.
- **Use your hands as a calming fence.** Stance is the embodiment of a physical attitude that is both non-confrontational yet ready for action. When facing an aggressive individual, stand with your hands clasped in front of your chest, the back of one hand in the palm of the other, palms inwards. This is the **strong conversation stance**. When the other person becomes agitated, you rotate your forearms so that the palms are out, slightly curved, as if you are intending to catch something. This is the **fence**. (When the person calms, you revert back to the **strong conversation stance**.)

  Fences lend a feeling of security.[1] Some of us lean on a fence to talk to our neighbor, but we also receive a sense of privacy and protection. Similarly, when you place both of your hands in front of you, palms out, you establish a boundary between you and the individual. The arms should angle from the body at about thirty degrees, and the hands should be relaxed and curved slightly. Were the individual to then come close enough

---

1   I owe the image of the hands as a fence to Geoff Thompson, brilliant writer who has authored a number of books on his career as a doorman in violent British pubs, as well as exemplary books on self-defense. While on the subject of Mr. Thompson, I must also recommend his fiction, both novels and plays, which are both powerful and sometimes heartbreaking.

that his or her body or hands touch yours, there is no doubt that they are intruding on your personal space. Upon making physical contact with you, most individuals will back off. If they do not, this means that they are either no longer aware of personal boundaries, or worse, they are about to attack. You can also use your upraised hands to push away or fend off the individual if you have to. Your hands should be relaxed, and

 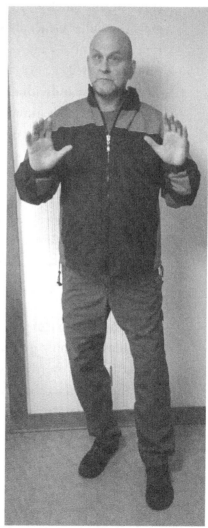

not clenched in a rigid, fighting posture. <u>Your hands and arms should express that you are closed off to physical contact, but open to listening.</u>

- **Do not touch the irritated person.** Do not touch people hoping to calm them down, unless you know them very well and they trust you <u>in that moment</u>, despite their anger. There are very few occasions where touching angry people will make the situation better. Such situations do exist with distraught children, but rarely with adults, and *particularly* not with aggressive adults. Generally speaking, the only time you should touch a potentially aggressive person should be when you must protect yourself.

- **Try to get the individual to sit rather than stand.** Pacing and stomping around is stimulating, and most people are more ready to fight when they are on their feet. Whenever possible, try and remain seated, and get the other person to sit as well. Should they repeatedly rise out of their chair, the situation is obviously escalating. If the individual stands, you should stand as well, because otherwise you are at an immediate disadvantage.

- **Let them leave if they want to**. Assaults frequently occur when the individual tries to disengage, but you insist on working things out *right now*. (This particularly occurs in family arguments). This is almost always a mistake, as the individual is leaving to try to calm down—or worse, they realize that if they stay, they will only get more furious. If the individual is too enraged, or has overtly threatened to commit an act of violence *after* they leave, let them leave and contact law enforcement.

Figure 7   How to improve your stance

Look at the photographs in this chapter. Imitate each of these stances in turn. Try to stand for five minutes. Notice if you are, by 'nature,' unbalanced. Is it hard to stand, relaxed, without moving for a few minutes. As a daily practice, simply stand in one or both of these postures, breathing smoothly. Rebalance yourself by relaxing your knees slightly, and standing with your weight evenly distributed in your feet. Don't lock your knees, or stand either back on your heels or on the balls of your feet.

It is very difficult to speak in a way that engenders respect when you are swaying like a tree in the wind, or shifting back and forth. As paradoxical a concept as it may seem, the more gracefully and quietly you can stand, the more effective your words will be.

CHAPTER 8

Tone And Quality Of Your Voice
For De-escalation

- **Use a Firm, Low Pitch.** Try to pitch your voice *slightly* lower than normal. 'Drop' your voice into your chest, so it resonates from the center of your body. This will make you feel calm as well as projecting a sense of strength to the other person. Do not betray any negative or angry emotions: a calm, low-pitched voice communicates to the individual that you are in control of yourself and therefore, the situation as well.

- **Slow Down.** In most cases, you should speak a little slower than the person you are trying to de-escalate. By slowing down just a little, you are trying to get them to resonate with your calmer pace, and also keeping yourself from being swept up in their energy.

- **Do not be condescending.** When communicating with an angry person, do not use a condescending or bored tone. Talking to adult individuals, even those with a mental illness, as if they were children or not worthy of respect, will cause them to become even more angry and agitated. One way many people unconsciously condescend to the other is rolling their eyes upwards to one side—In every culture I have ever encountered, this means "I hold you in contempt." If you do the 'eye-roll,' you will have an angry person in front of you, no matter what you are saying.

- **The use of a dramatic voice.** Sometimes, particularly with someone with a 'child-like' affect, the best tactic is to use a dramatic voice, loud and somewhat enthusiastic, using charisma to grab attention. Make your voice a little louder, and use charisma to grab attention.

Figure 8.1 Example: The Dramatic Voice

An upset woman, perhaps suffering from a mental illness or developmental disability, is upset because she thinks people in the utility company lobby are laughing at her. You know her and also know that she has never been physically threatening to anyone at your business. You come out from behind the reception desk and say, "Claire, I SEE you are upset! I'D be upset too if I thought people were laughing at me! Now COME ON over here!" Indicate with your body where you want her to go, moving as if you are absolutely certain she will comply. "C'mon. I want you to tell me EXACTLY what happened—EVERY word! Let's go over here where no one can bother us!" You show her that not only are you giving her your complete attention, but the drama means that she is important, someone worth listening to. By moving her somewhere else to talk, you remove her from the scene that is upsetting her.

I sometimes refer to this as my 'Sesame Street' voice—by this I mean a voice that is somewhat loud, even boisterous, but harmless as well, like one of the cuddly monsters on that TV show. It is particularly helpful when dealing with someone who is, due to their disabilities, somewhat childlike. This is not patronizing—it is a way of getting the attention of someone who will not be able to track a 'serious' voice, and who will be either frightened or angered by a 'command voice' (just like a child who is throwing a tantrum).

- **Verbal commands.** You will sometimes find that a lower-pitched voice will not grab and hold the individual's attention. For an individual who is very disorganized or angry, the use of a low-pitched voice will not be effective, as it will not penetrate through the fog of their hysteria or agitation. When necessary, give the individual a clear, firm, and strong command (not yelling) to cease and desist. Do not yell shrilly or with a pleading tone. Be firm and authoritative, letting the individual know that you are in command.

- **The Battle Cry.** There are almost no situations where you should be yelling at the individual. There is one exception: when the individual is moving toward you to attack, or is otherwise presenting immediate danger to another, you should roar like a lion to startle and freeze the individual's motion momentarily with commands like "STAY BACK" or "STEP AWAY," so you can evade, counter, or escape. The way you do this is as follows:

  1. Open your eyes WIDE!
  2. Slam your stomach BACK-WARDS, trying to connect your navel and your spine.
  3. Tighten your throat. (This can leave with a raw throat for the next day, but it's worth it if it saves you or someone else from harm.)
  4. ROAR a command.

Figure 8.2 Wording in a Battle Cry

When someone is moving towards you with hostile intent, do not command that they "STOP." They may do what you say, yet still be too close to you. Command that they "STEP BACK" or "MOVE BACK."

The command "STOP" is used to arrest an action that will, <u>in itself</u>, result in harm. For example, if the person is about to jump in front of a car, or throw something.

CHAPTER 9

Across The Spectrum
Of Anger

Figure 9.1 IMPORTANT: Methods Used to De-escalate Angry People Do Not Work With <u>Enraged</u> People
In fact, they will very likely further escalate the situation. Imagine trying to 'validate' a berserk methamphetamine-intoxicated psychotic, "I see you want to smash the windows of my car with that piece of wood. Thank you for being so clear in expressing your intentions."

Conversely, using strategies that are suitable for enraged people (control tactics) with merely irritated or angry people will flame them upwards *into* rage. Imagine coming home and your spouse tells you that he or she is not happy that you forgot the groceries in the trunk of the car, and you say, "Step back. Step back right now!"

Y ou must first center yourself before attempting to de-escalate an angry person. (See Section VII below—if you properly practice the material in this section, centering will become an automatic, almost instantaneous act.) You can say all the right things, but if you are not centered and calm yourself, your words will have no effect.

From a position of calm strength, calm them. If you do not establish safety for yourself and others, you can be of no assistance to the individual, or anyone else. This does not mean that you should not talk with a person while they are upset. What I mean is that everything you do and say must have a tactical basis, in the service of establishing safety and peace. In the sections that follow, the reader will be introduced to a variety of de-escalation techniques. Some are applicable over a wide range of circumstances, whereas others may only be useful in very specific situations. Think of them like the scales and octaves of music that must be mastered so that you can improvise freely.

- **Trust your Hunches.** If you have a vague sense that something is wrong with the individual, you are probably right. Be proactive—the earlier you intervene in a problem, the less likelihood there will be that it gets out of control.

- **Authoritative Presence.** Your presence may be enough to calm an individual down. 'Presence,' however, does not merely mean that you are 'filling space.' It means that you have established, through your demeanor, that you possess an authority that cannot be ignored.

- **Be what you want them to be.** Speak to them calmly, control your breathing, and maintain an upright and non-threatening posture, all the while remaining ready to respond to any attack. They become calmer in reaction to your calm.

- **Watchful Waiting.** A crisis always requires a moment-by-moment decision on the best course of action. It is occasionally best that you remain centered and ready, as the individual calms down without any assistance from anyone else. Sometimes the best de-escalation tactic is letting them control themselves.

- **One Point of Contact.** When de-escalating an individual, only one person should be communicating with them. This becomes more relevant the angrier they become. Trying to talk to two or more people at once, particularly if *they* are not in complete agreement, will cause the angry individual to become more and more confused, as well as making him/her feel surrounded and overwhelmed.

- **De-escalate—then solve the problem**. <u>You cannot solve a problem with an angry person</u>. Remember, the individual sees the conflict as a win-lose proposition. They will view any negotiation or agreement as a loss of power. For this reason, <u>first eliminate the anger, and then engage in problem-solving</u>.
- **When to use humor**. This ability to see a situation from another perspective can *sometimes* work like magic. However, be careful! It only is helpful when the other person is *somewhat* irritated, rather than in a state of strong anger. If they are too upset or agitated, their response to a joke or humorous comment is likely to be, "You think this is a joke? You are making fun of me?"

Figure 9.2   Humor is not always Disarming

I once brought a man to an emergency room after he overdosed on his medications. He was a little guy, usually very gentle, suffering from bipolar disorder. Dressed in pajamas, with his thin hair in disarray, he looked like a very confused little bird.

The hospital gave him charcoal and an emetic, the first to absorb the medications, and the second to get it out of his body. He was sitting on a gurney with a vomit pan in his hand, and in between retches, he was talking a mile a minute (a manifestation of his illness), saying, "Why do you give me mediations like this. RETCH I can't be trusted. I'm not very responsible. Why don't you give me Skittles? RETCH Chase the rainbow! RETCH At least I won't have to come here and RETCH go through this."

One of the nurses in attendance reacted as if he was consciously trying to be funny. He certainly sounded that way! In fact, this was a manifestation of nervousness and agitation. She made a joke about the rainbow he was retching, and he suddenly picked up his head and said, "Funny? I said something funny? Nothing's funny!" And which point he Frisbee'd the vomit pan across the room, gouts of black fluid going everywhere (sorry reader, but as gross as that sounds, imagine being there!).

And all learned a lesson—humor only is useful as a calming tactic when people are *slightly* agitated.

- **Do not try to win. Try to establish peace.** Try to resolve the situation so that the individual can separate from you with his or her pride intact. Even if they have not achieved their original goal, the individual should at least have a certain amount of respect for the way that you handled the situation.

CHAPTER 10

Diamonds In The Rough: Essential Strategies For The De-Escalation Of Anger

Codes For Living: Following The Access Route

People often have a code by which they live. Some of those codes are based on the culture into which they are born, and others are based on their profession or lifestyle, or something they developed on their own. The heart of their code is often a phrase or a couple of words that sums up their deepest values. When people talk about themselves, their codes of living are often woven throughout their speech—this is especially so when an angry person's reason for outrage is their belief that his or her code is being threatened:

- They perceive that others are demanding they violate their code.
- They take offense when others do not conform to their code.
- Another's actions require them to respond, lest they violate their code.

Angry individuals will very often proclaim their values and code for living in their explanation or tirade. You should be able to identify their core metaphor in one or two words or phrases.

Figure 10.1 Expressions That Reflect a Code for Living

Person one. "I'm a man. He can't talk about me that way."

Person two. "Think of how I feel. If someone did that to you, wouldn't you be upset?"

Person three. "Are you saying I'm not going to get my medical coverage extended? It doesn't matter what HR says! I worked here 27 years. I did the job. You are not cutting me off just because of some new rule. You owe me!"

Person four. "I was standing there all alone. Everyone was looking at me. Talking about me!"

You should be able to describe their code in one or two words. What is most important to each of these people in the above examples? The first person's is pride; the second is caring for others or empathy; for the third, it is mutual obligation; and the fourth person is fearful of being humiliated.

The code is an access route to the individual. When you incorporate it in your response, you are recognizing the individual's values (however misguided or anti-social they may be). This is what many people mean by the term 'respect'—that you recognize his or her code and take it into account. The connection you thereby establish, however tenuous, allows you to work with the individual toward a resolution. For example:

- If you discern that personal integrity is a core issue of concern, frame your responses and suggestions with the same theme. "I wouldn't want people talking about you as a man who can't control himself."

- To the young individual who believes someone treated him with disrespect: "Man, I can see how angry you are. I'd be angry too if someone said that to me, but if you try to hurt him, you'll end up losing your job. Yeah, I know you think he *disrespected* you, but if you assault him, you would be letting him *own* you. He says three words, and your response means you lose your place here, where you have got a fine future. Is that what you want?"
- Sometimes a core metaphor is situational, something as ostensibly benign as the weather. "Look, Frank, it's a hot day, I'm tired, and I guess you are too. I don't care who's right here, really. I just want to finish my drink and get on my way. Damn, these days are nasty. Here we are, all stressed out just because we're both hot and tired."

Limit Setting

Limit setting is most often used when you are in a position of authority—or you simply **'step up' and take an authoritative position**. Remember, though, as soon as you draw a line, it will become the main focus of your interchange. Only set limits that the person can actually do. Do not ever set a limit that you cannot enforce or one that is not reasonable and simple to understand. Your tone of voice should be matter-of-fact, rather than critical. Simply remind them of the rule or set a proper limit. Remember though, that limit setting is the act of consciously drawing a line that the other person is not to cross. For better or for worse, it is a confrontation—sometimes it is absolutely necessary, but there's no going back once you've chosen this strategy.

Silence

Sometimes, the most powerful thing you can do is to be silent. Be sure that you are not being passive-aggressive, fuming in silent anger, or appearing to ignore or dismiss the person. Instead, you should wait: quietly and powerfully. Keep your facial expressions calm, your posture centered, and carefully listen. Nod your head calmly as you listen, doing so slowly and intermittently. In many cultures, including the United States, nodding your head too rapidly indicates that you want the other person to hurry up and finish, or worse, just shut up.

Silence, however, is not that easy, particularly if you are suffering the brunt of another's anger. There are three ways to listen silently, and two of them will make people angrier than before.

- **Contemptuous Silence.** You are tired of the dispute, or tired of the individual. You fidget, you sigh, and you roll your eyes to one side, and twist one corner of your mouth. In almost every culture, this facial expression and behaviors express an attitude of contempt, and is guaranteed to provoke anger or rage.

- **Stonewall Silence.** When you stonewall, you ignore the individual, or otherwise make it clear that you wish they would shut up. Your demeanor shows that you have no interest in what they have to say or why they are saying it. You can do this inadvertently by entering notes into your computer, watching a TV screen, or by taking a phone call during the conversation. Stonewalling can evoke anxiety or anger in the individual who wants to communicate, only to find that there's a 'wall' in the way. As a result, they will do anything to 'get through to you,' including trying to tear down that wall.

  In addition to upsetting the individual, such indifferent behaviors will also decrease your ability to defend yourself from attack because your attention is focused elsewhere instead of where it should be: on the aggressor.

- **The right way to listen: Interested Silence.** When you have been truly listening, the aggressive person often interrupts his or her own tirade to ask, "Aren't you going to say something?" That is your opportunity to move in and direct the situation.

  You may have to interrupt them if they don't stop themselves, and simply continue to talk and talk. Do this by advancing a hand slightly a little above waist level, fingers curved, palms down (you don't want the individual to interpret your hand movement as a 'shut up' gesture). You should also lean toward the individual slightly, indicating that it's your turn to speak. If they don't notice your hand gesture, put both hands up in front of you in a 'fence' (Chapter 7) and tell them to stop a moment, in a voice that is loud and holds a little humor. "Joey, Joey, wait a minute. You gotta give me a chance to say something! Listen to me a second!"

After interrupting the individual, the first thing you should do is to sum up your understanding of what he/she just said. This proves that you are indeed listening to them, and are interested in solving their problem. Once you have summed it up, you can either go into problem solving-mode, or, if they are still heated, shift into 'tactical paraphrasing' (Chapter 11).

Figure 10.2 Silence

She has been talking for ten minutes. You had called her in to your office to discuss a performance issue at work, and she launches into a story about all her troubles at home: with her child, her partner, and her parents. After one attempt to focus on the issue at hand, she becomes dramatic, emotional and more upset. Even trying to validate her upset upsets her more, because she takes it as you interrupting before she has said everything she needs to say.

After ten minutes, however, she shows no sign of stopping, so you hold up two hands, fingers and palms a little curved, like you are catching a thrown object, and you say, "Maureen. Just a moment." And you put a little drama in your voice, and say, "This is very important! What you are saying is very important, but I have to tell you something!"

She pauses, and the first thing you do is sum up what she said. "You and I began talking about some work that wasn't prepared to your usual standards, a small thing. But you told me that there's a context to this. Your child is having trouble at school. Your father, who lives with you, says that it is your fault because you work and are not at home (even though you are supporting your family, *including* him, and your partner's COBRA has run out and her medical bills are not going away. *(You have proved you were listening through tactical paraphrasing, described in Chapter 11, and then you SET A LIMIT).* I don't want you to talk any more about this though, for two reasons: You have told me enough for me to understand <u>why</u> your performance is different from usual. The second reason is this—you need to talk to the right person about this. You are telling me very personal information about things I cannot help. I know it's rough, and that's why you need to talk to HR and to EAP to get some help, be it consultation on your partner's medical situation or some counseling, just so you have someone to talk to about this. Maureen, thank you. Because you shared this with me, you helped me understand that you need to talk to the right people to get help with this. But we have to return to one more thing *(open ended question)*—"Given your current family situation, what do you need to do to make sure you return to your former standards and finish your work without errors?"

Note here, how silence is a 'gateway strategy,' which allows you to then use others: tactical paraphrasing, limit setting, problem solving and open-ended questioning.

Break The Pattern

You may find yourself in the same argument(s) over and over again, and often with different individuals! In order to detect any patterns or behaviors that may have affected your communication with an individual negatively, you can easily perform an 'After Action Review' of you own actions and responses in past disputes, noting your 'hot buttons,' (Chapter 34). An honest attempt at self-reflection may reveal patterns of behavior, personal style, even personal codes, that have had a detrimental effect on your interaction with a particular individual, or group of similar individuals.

There is another type of pattern, however, one that is imposed upon you. For example, here are three possible interchanges with the same aggressor:

Interchange #1:
Aggressor – "What are you looking at?"

You – "Nothing"

Aggressor – "You are calling me nothing?

Interchange #2:
Aggressor – "What are you looking at?"

You – "I was just looking in your direction. I didn't mean anything by it."

Aggressor – "You were looking at me? There's a problem with my face? Are you calling me ugly?"

Interchange #3:
Aggressor – "What are you looking at?"

You – "I was just looking around the room."

Aggressor – "Are you playing games with me? Around the room? You were looking right at me!"

Using some slang that is probably older than many of my readers, the aggressor is putting you in a 'trick bag' – no matter what you do, he'll make a fight out of it.

In situations like this, you may be forced to more dramatically break the pattern of interaction between you and an individual, by doing or saying something that makes continuing the dispute absolutely impossible. In many cases, you will use a dramatic voice or display somewhat uncharacteristic or unexpected behaviors. This technique is not recommended for 'routine' episodes of de-escalation, and most definitely not as an opening in any encounter. However, breaking the pattern can be effective because many individuals expect their targets to react in a somewhat predictable manner to their displays of anger and/ or violence. By reacting in an unanticipated manner, you can throw the individual off balance. This tactic can even work with very angry individuals. It sometimes takes the fight out of the interchange, like suddenly letting out the air from a tire.

Determining the time and necessity of breaking the pattern may seem like magic, but instead, this is an intuitive skill that is developed with time and experience. You certainly cannot prepare an array of specialized catch-phrases ready to disarm an aggressive individual. This technique is pure improvisation, but it is grounded in the same strong and powerful calm that I have written about throughout this manual. If you consciously try to be overly creative, or if you are excited about what a cool or funny thing you are about to say, it may indeed be something witty, but it will be at the wrong time, to the wrong individual. And things will get worse. When you are in control of yourself, with the mainline skills of de-escalation at hand, such improvisation will simply emerge.

Figure 10.2   Breaking the Pattern

Breaking the Pattern #1

A young woman found herself in a dangerous neighborhood, walking towards a bus stop, with several men approaching her with sleazy comments. They surrounded her and started to 'herd' her towards a park. She suddenly started to cackle in high shrieks, pulled her hair to each side of her head and flapped it like wings. The men pulled back in shock, because she was the strangest, weirdest looking being they had ever seen outside their own nightmares. She stepped quickly between two of them into the street, dodged a car, and went into an all-night store, cackling and shrieking until she got inside, where she called a friend to pick her up. (NOTE: Some people find even imagining acting like this to be embarrassing, but consider, acting 'crazy,' maybe even bonking yourself on the head once or twice, is certainly better than being a victim of violence).

Breaking the Pattern #2

An elderly woman was accosted by a somewhat drunk, very large man on a winter's night as she was walking back to her car. As he lurched towards her, she took the initiative. Taking off her coat, the tiny woman looked up at the man and said, "My goodness. You look cold. Here, take my coat." He blearily looked at her and said, "What?" She continued, "It is a terrible night. I have grandchildren your age, you shouldn't be cold like that" and she pushed the coat, impossibly small at the man. He stepped back and said, "I couldn't take your coat. I couldn't do that. I couldn't even fit in your coat. You should go home, lady. The streets aren't safe around here."

Breaking the Pattern #3

An acquaintance of mine was in Germany when the Berlin Wall fell. He was walking with two friends from Morocco, both of whom had darker-than-German skin. They were in a plaza and suddenly a group of drunken neo-Nazi's marched towards them, shouting racist curses. The three men backed up against a fountain, prepared to fight to survive, and my friend suddenly jumped up on the edge of the fountain and started singing Broadway show tunes, complete with soft-shoe dance routines along the edge of the fountain. He must have sung four verses, the drunken men staring at him with their mouths open (as were his Moroccan friends). He stopped, threw his hands open and like a Mel Brooks movie, the leader of the pack started applauding, followed by all of his cohorts. They picked up the three of them up, carried them on their shoulders and off they all went to a night of drinking.

CHAPTER 11

Tactical Paraphrasing:
The Gold Standard With
Angry Individuals

What Is Paraphrasing?

Paraphrasing is perhaps the most important technique for calming <u>angry</u> individuals. You sum up in a phrase or sentence <u>your understanding</u> of what they have just said in a paragraph. If you paraphrase accurately, you have established that you have 'gotten' it that far, so they do not have to repeat it, or try to say it in other words. It is like peeling off a single layer of an onion so that you can be shown the next layer. If you do not demonstrate that you 'get' it, the individual will feel compelled to repeat and/or elaborate that layer of their anger with more and more intensity. As they get more intense, they usually get more irrational, and their ability to communicate breaks down even further. The wonderful thing about paraphrasing is that you do not have to be 'smart' and interpret anything. You simply have to listen and inform them of what you understand.

Returning to our image of an onion, as you peel off each layer, they get to the next layer that is driving them. A very intense man might start out complaining about his son being late for this appointment they were supposed to attend together [and that paraphrased], he tells you that he is afraid his son will lose his job, due to his attitude [and that paraphrased], he tells you that his wife left him and the family is falling apart

Paraphrasing establishes that you are truly listening and have understood what they have said. There is another component, however, where we take a slightly activist approach. We SELECT what we will sum up from the complex, multi-faceted communication that the individual has just given us, <u>choosing the healthiest aspect of what they have just said.</u>

This method is 'self-correcting,' whereas passive 'reflection' (sometimes called 'mirroring') can make things worse. If you sum up an angry person's worst impulses, they will find themselves in agreement with you. If you sum up an aspect of what they have said that is in the direction of conflict resolution, you will draw out of them that part of them that DOES wish to resolve the conflict. On the other hand, if they are, in fact, bent on mayhem, they will correct you by escalating what they are saying, believing that you are not getting the message. <u>Remember, they are trying to communicate</u>! All you have to do is sum up what you understand from what they said. When you get it right, they go to the next layer.

Figure 11.1 Example of Correct and Incorrect Paraphrasing

Angry Father. I'm so mad at my daughter that I could just wring her neck!"

Incorrect paraphrase: "You want to murder your daughter."

Correct paraphrase: "You are furious with her!"

If you have, in the second example, accurately paraphrased the meaning of the angry father's intention, you will naturally go on to the next layer of his complaint.

***Angry* Father.** "You won't believe what she did. I come home and find her on the couch lip-locking that punk from down the street. You know, the kid who epoxies his hair in spikes?"

If, however, the second example is *inaccurate*, the angry father will correct you with more vehemence.

Angry Father. "No, not 'really upset.' I honestly intend to loop a belt around her neck and slowly strangle her. Seriously! She better not come home tonight. I will kill her."

At which point you will call law enforcement.

Why would he confess his intent in the second example? Remember that one of the hallmark qualities of angry people is that they are trying to communicate. He started talking to you, and when you misunderstood, it is a natural thing for him to correct you so that you 'get' what he is saying. I am not saying that people will always confess a future crime. I am saying that paraphrasing is the best way to talk with angry people who are trying to make you understand what they are upset about.

Why Not Simply Ask the Person What's Going On? If They Want To Tell Me Something, Why Don't They Just Answer The Questions?

Asking questions is usually not a good idea with really angry individuals. They already believe you have to 'get' what they are saying, and a question shows that you do not. Now frustrated at their failure to make you understand, this makes them try harder and louder, albeit with less coherence than before. Your question means, as far as they are concerned, that they cannot get through to you! When anger is combined with a sense of powerlessness, the individual feels like he/she is 'losing' to a more powerful other. In essence, they experience a question as a demand for an answer, putting you in a dominant position.

Figure 11.2 The Problem With Questions

You surely have experienced how irritating questions can be. Imagine coming home after a bad day. You are hot, tired, and frustrated. You walk into your house, drop your gear on the floor, sigh loudly, and walk toward the shower. Your spouse says, "Did you have a bad day?" Isn't this irritating? Isn't it *obvious* you've had a bad day? After all these years together, and he/she doesn't know when a bad day just walked into the house!

On the other hand, imagine your spouse observing you, then saying, "Bad day, huh?" You continue walking towards the shower, and say, "I don't want to talk now. I just want a shower. I'll talk to you later." You are not 'forced' to explain yourself.

How To Use Paraphrasing Successfully

The following will help you in paraphrasing successfully:
- It is very important that your voice is strong and calm. You speak to the individual as someone who has the power within to take care of his/her problem, not as someone who is fragile or volatile (even if he/she is). Speak to their strength.
- Sometimes, you can use a dramatic summation, "You are really ticked off!" Here, you sum up the individual's mood with your voice and posture, in addition to what is being said.

Reaching The Core Level Of The Problem

We know we have reached the core level when there is no more 'progress.' The individual **spins his wheels**. They may use different words, but they say essentially the same thing over and over again. For example, after you have paraphrased a number of things that the person has said during his angry tirade, he says:

- "I'm just so tired of this whole situation" – and after you paraphrase that, he says:
- "It's gotten so old. Nothing changes"—and after you paraphrase that, he says:
- "Every day it's the same thing"

Obviously, you are spinning wheels together—you've hit the core level of the problem, at least for now.

Other people express relief at being finally understood; some individuals exhibit an intensification of emotion, because you have reached that which is most distressing.

- With some individuals, you have, by paraphrasing them every step of the way, established that you are a person of trust. In some cases, you can now be quite directive, telling them what you think they should do, because we often are willing to accept advice or even instruction from people we trust.
- With others, we are ready to engage in a collaborative process of problem-solving, trying to figure out a way to solve the situation that is in the best interest of everyone involved. You start problem solving with a **summation of the core problem.** This helps both of you establish that you've understood the situation correctly. Then you **try to put the problem solving back into their hands with you as a collaborator, someone on their side**. For example, starting with the summation: "You have been here seven years, and you love the work. Jackley has shown contempt for the organization since the day of his hire. We are aware that material has been stolen, and we are quite sure that it is him. But he claims, despite the evidence, that it was you. I do understand your code about not 'snitching.' But

I also understand that another part of your code is that a man owns up to his own sins and stands up for himself. From what you've said, seems to me that you are only honoring half of your code. We have to figure out a way that we can clear this up without feeling that you have violated a code that Jackley does not even believe in. "

Do Not Waste It

Paraphrasing is almost a cliché, so much so that I can imagine some of you rolling your eyes when you read the title of this chapter. This technique is too important to abandon, and at the same time, it must be used carefully: that is, <u>rarely</u>. If the individual is not really angry, simply talk with them, using some of the other strategies in the previous chapters in this section.

If there is a crisis, however, <u>and</u> the individual does *not* believe they are understood, paraphrasing comes into its own. Paraphrasing can have an almost electrifying effect with an angry individual. Imagine the feeling when you try to pull a splinter from under your fingernail, and after ten long minutes of aggravating struggle, you get a hold of it finally and pull it out of your nail bed. That is the sense you get when, angry and desperate to be heard, you realize that the other person 'got it.'

Figure 11.3   How to master paraphrasing so that you can actually use it in an emergency

A similar technique, often called 'active listening' is probably the most commonly suggested strategy in dealing with aggressive people. However, this technique is usually taught so that you are required to use a rather stilted way of talking that is oddly 'distancing. ' For example"

- "So what you are sharing with me is . . ."
- "What I hear you saying is . . ."

Few people really *want* to talk like that, and in emergencies, you *can't* talk like that! When you are hit by adrenaline, you will stumble over your words because that way of talking is unnatural to you.

So, don't do this! Most people will find you irritating, and you will be 'in your head' at a time where you must be aware of what's going on in front of you.

You are, in fact, a master of paraphrasing. You do it all the time, simply keeping a conversation going, saying things like:

1. To an unhappy parent—"Your kid flunked out, huh?"
2. To a fellow employee—"You're not getting a raise."
3. To your neighbor, who is complaining about someone down the block—"You hate that guy."
4. To your friend who has just fallen in love—"She's the one."

In short, the natural statements you intersperse in any conversation are perfect paraphrasing. However, because you do this unconsciously, it's hard to tap into as an *emergency technique*. It's easy to perfect, however. Consider this—how many conversations do you have a day? Twenty? Thirty? WELL, HERE'S YOUR HOMEWORK. In each and every conversation, at an arbitrary moment of your choosing, decide to paraphrase the next thing they say. Just once. They won't even notice. But because you made a conscious decision to do this, *your brain notices.*

That means you have successfully practiced that skill twenty to forty times a day, and you know you are doing it. Rather than a reflex, it's a choice. Consider how good any skill would be if you do twenty repetitions a day, with each one a total success! With this method, you will be able to step into crisis-oriented paraphrasing without hesitation. It will be so natural to you that you do not even have to think about it.

CHAPTER 12

Big Mistakes That Seem
Like Such Good Ideas
At The Time

De-escalation requires improvisation in a very fluid and dynamic situation, often with volatile and unpredictable individuals. In such a highly charged atmosphere, where clear communication is necessary to prevent any misunderstandings, you must think quickly, but calmly, before speaking. By maintaining an emotional distance, and not reacting personally to anything the individual may say, you will be less likely to escalate an already heated situation.

Nonetheless, we make mistakes, even the best of us. As an old Japanese proverb puts it, "Even monkeys fall from trees." Many of our mistakes are very obvious, and the moment something leaves our mouth, we think, "Uh-oh. I shouldn't have said that!" This can be prevented rather easily by taking a moment to gather your thoughts before responding to what the individual has said. Sometimes you can hold up your hands to give them pause, gather your own resources, and then reply.

Other mistakes are subtler. On certain days, you may be tired, not feeling well, or are distracted by family matters perhaps, and de-escalating an angry individual is the last thing you wish to do. Not surprisingly, risk increases when you are at less than your optimum ability and awareness. Your timing will be off, you will choose the wrong wording for what you intend to say, and you will be off-center. You actually need to be more alert and in control of yourself on occasions when you are not at your best.

The following topics are areas to be aware of, so as not to make a mistake that leads to an escalating encounter with an angry individual:

Ingratiation (Sucking Up)

Do not try to ingratiate yourself with the individual. Do not ignore aggressive behavior in the hopes that the person will eventually calm down on their own.

One of the paradoxes of ingratiation is that people who allow the aggressor to control their interactions often claim they have a 'special rapport' with them—a person who, in fact, intimidates them. Oddly enough, these same 'conflict-avoidant' people are often suppressing a lot of anger at being controlled. They displace this on those who point out to them what they are doing. Thus, one of the first signs that a person is ingratiating is an attitude of self-righteousness, a defense mechanism that enables them to avoid questioning violating their own integrity. The following factors are also signs of ingratiation:

- You worry about 'how things are going' between yourself and the aggressor, and act or react on that basis.
- You are sometimes ashamed of your actions, or believe that you are acting in a cowardly fashion.
- You believe you are caring and nice, and react with shocked outrage when the aggressor is unkind, cruel, or disrespectful toward you, as if you and that person had made some sort of transaction that they have now betrayed.
- You allow the other person to speak to you in overly familiar or rude terms, such as dude, buddy, pal, babe, sweetheart, etc.

The Mistake Of Mind Reading

Sometimes, people will try to connect with an aggressive person by telling them how they must feel, by confessing to having the same issues, or claiming to have gone through a similar situation. Statements like, "I know how you feel," or "I know you love this job," are statements that the angry individual may not agree with at all. You have tried to usurp their issue. They then decide to prove you wrong by demonstrating that they are NOT what you just said they are.

The Mistake Of Allowing Venting

Venting is an expression of energy, such as going for a run after a difficult day, or chopping wood until fatigued so that you can let go of an unpleasant incident. However, tantrums and tirades are also designated by this same term.

Letting an individual 'get something off their chest' is not the same as venting. The purpose of the former action is to get finished with something by talking about it. The purpose of venting is to stoke oneself up to higher levels of aggression.

Many people have a false idea about aggression and imagine it to be some kind of psychological fluid that builds up pressure within us. When we vent (hence the word), these people believe that we get rid of the anger and then become peaceful, similar to a valve releasing pressure from a water line. But aggression is not a fluid; it is a state of arousal. Just like any other state of arousal—sexuality, happiness, excited interest—additional stimuli elicit more arousal. When a person shouts, yells, complains or kicks things, they are stimulating themselves to greater and greater aggression. Therefore, if you allow an individual to vent angrily, the more aroused, and hence, angry they become. This only makes de-escalation more difficult.

When you let an individual vent about other people, they perceive that you are giving implicit approval to their verbal complaints and abuse. However, if they get so angry that they start to become dangerous and *then* you object, they will turn on you, asserting, "You are on their side!" Thus, if an individual begins to vent, consider it an act of self-arousal, not a decompression of internal tension. De-escalate and control them instead.

Obvious Mistakes We Should Not Make, But Do Anyway

Although some of the items included in the following list have been discussed before in this book, they are repeated here as a reminder to the reader of the seemingly minor, yet crucial, details of de-escalation.

- **Don't' make threats or promise consequences you cannot keep.** The failure to follow through on promises made or consequences threatened will also serve to undermine your authority or creditability with the individual after the incident has been resolved.

- **Don't bombard the individual with too many choices, questions, and solutions**. This will only overwhelm them, especially if they are suffering from mental illness, emotional disturbance or intoxication.

- **Don't ask an upset individual, "Why?"** Asking a 'why' question demands an answer or an explanation from the individual, something they may be quite unwilling, or unable, to do.

- **Don't talk down to the individual as if they were stupid or ignorant, or, conversely, in an overly solicitous manner**. Do not roll your eyes or sigh heavily while the individual is trying to communicate with you. Generally, do not interrupt as they speak, particularly to correct what they are saying. On the other hand, interruption of aggressive verbalizations or pointless monologues IS the right thing to do.

- **Don't analyze their behavior while trying to de-escalate them**. Don't tell people why they think and feel the things they do.

- **Don't share the individual's private information in front of others.** This will cause them to feel shamed and humiliated.
- **Don't' take things personally when the individual attacks your character or professionalism.** The measure of a person of integrity is NOT taking things personally.
- **Don't allow the individual to trespass on your personal boundaries.**
- **Don't touch, push, or try to forcefully move the individual from one place to another, or point at them in a threatening manner.** The only time when you should put your hands on an aggressive individual is in the rare event when you are defending yourself physically, or, if it is your <u>professional</u> responsibility to physically move an individual from one area to another, or off the premises.
- **Don't adopt an authoritarian or demeaning attitude, particularly in front of their peers or other onlookers.** Authoritarian attitudes and behaviors are some of the most common precipitants of assault by individuals.

Figure 12   If you've made a mistake – apologize!

It is often very difficult to apologize in the face of aggression. Anger always justifies itself, so if we are angered by the way we perceive the other as treating us, admitting we made a mistake is hard to do, or even realize. We are also afraid, at times, that the aggressor will take this as a sign of weakness or use it as leverage.

I once backed out of my driveway, without turning my head far enough and didn't see a car coming down the street. In rapid succession, I heard an enraged curse (his window was open), a car horn, a squeal of tires, and then a thump as he avoided my car by jumping a curb onto the side of the road.

He was screaming like a scalded cat as he jumped out of his car. I did not want to be sitting in my seat as he ran up to the window so I jumped out of my car as well. He was screaming that his wife and children were in the car, and I could have killed them. In the loudest voice I could, I yelled, "Are they OK? Your wife? Your kids? Are they OK?" He yelled, "Yeah, no thanks to you, you could have . . ." I held up both hands (both in defense, because he had his fists clenched and also to interrupt) and said, "Listen to me. This was my fault! My fault! I am so sorry I caused this, and so glad your family is alright." His breathing slowed, but he wanted to continue berating me, but as he started cursing again, I interrupted, and said, firmly and slowly, "I meant it. I'm not just saying words. I'm sorry. Your kids have been through enough. They shouldn't see us in a fight. Go back to your family, man. I'm sorry this ruined their day." He cursed at me one more time, turned around, got back in his car and drove away.

SECTION IV

Managing Rage

CHAPTER 13

Preface To Rage

Rage and anger are not merely different in degree; they are different modes of being, just as water, once past the boiling point, becomes steam. Frustrated people posture or otherwise act angrily to establish dominance, or to force compliance from others. If nothing else, their goal is to communicate . . . something . . . .

The reader will recall that anger is denoted as falling between 20 and 95 on the aggressiveness scale (Chapter 3). This represents a very broad range of behavior. Rage however, occupies a much smaller fraction of the scale, from 95 to 99. When in a state of rage, the individual <u>desires</u> to commit mayhem. They are in a 'threshold' state, escalating until they have overcome any moral or personal constraints that may prohibit them from committing the ultimate expression of aggression—violence.

Figure 13 The Use of Symbols

Here, and in several other areas of this book, I use animal symbols to aid in the understanding of various types of rage or other behavior. For example, I use the image of a leopard or a shark in describing predatory rage. These are thought devices, and are not intended to be used in either paperwork or communication to describe such individuals. In our hypersensitive times, such a reference may be misconstrued as stigmatizing an individual as 'being like an animal.' Nothing could be further from the truth; the images are to assist in understanding modes of behavior, not character. Nonetheless, such images should remain aids of understanding, not terms of reference.

I want to be very clear: all of the strategies described in the previous chapters for dealing with the angry individual are <u>useless</u> with one who is truly enraged. <u>You need other strategies entirely</u>. After reading this section of the book, you will be able to easily identify what type of rage the individual is exhibiting, and apply the appropriate strategies to control them.[2]

2   I owe a debt for some of the basic information in this section to a form of training called PART, thanks to a workshop I attended approximately 35 years ago. I have made major changes in their basic schema, as well as adding a significant amount of new data. My approach is, in many aspects, quite different, and it should not be confused with PART's procedures. Furthermore, what is in this book is an abbreviated version of my methodology for response to enraged people—my other books, written for people who must regularly deal with such individuals as well as those suffering from mental illness, offer far more extensive information.

CHAPTER 14

Terrified Rage

You may think that you will never be in a dangerous situation with someone in a terrified rage state, that something like that is probably confined to people in psychiatric hospitals or jails. However, sometimes children become terrified—if you have ever had a child who has 'night terrors,' then you know exactly what I mean. Also, those suddenly put in fear of their life—for example, a crime victim or victim of an auto accident—can sometime drop into a terrified state so extreme that they believe that the people trying to help them are dangerous to them. Therefore, although it is certainly not something most of us face every day or even every year (!), it is good to know how to respond if you are in such a situation.

What Do Individuals In Terrified Rage States Look Like?

Terrified individuals believe that they will be violated or abused. They appear apprehensive and furtive, looking halfway ready to run, halfway ready to strike. Their voice can be pleading, whiny or fearful, and their eyes are often wide-open or darting from place to place. However, wide-open eyes do not always indicate fear. When fearful, the muscles under the eyes are slack, giving the face a pleading look. Even though the terrified individual is looking in your direction, they do not, usually, look *into* your eyes, nor do they want you to look into theirs. Enraged-aggressive individuals, however, will stare penetratingly into your eyes or *through* you. In this case, their wide-open eyes will display tension all around the eyes, rather than the pleading look that terrified people display.

The mouths of some terrified individuals gape open slightly, as they breathe in panicky, short gasps, while others press their lips together in a quivering pucker. Their skin tone is often ashen or pale. Some make threatening gestures with a flailing overhand blow, while others primarily use a fending off gesture, as if trying to ward off attack. Their body posture can be described as concave, as they pull away from you or huddle tightly in fear. Terrified individuals also exhibit heightened levels of physical arousal, accompanied by panting, sweating, or trembling. They may back themselves into a wall or corner. They also may yell, seeming to be threatening and pleading simultaneously, using such phrases as, "Stay back! You get away from me! I will hit you!! I will! You stay back!" There is a hollow quality to their voices, as if  it has no 'foundation.' This is due to the tightening of their abdomen and diaphragm, so that not only their breathing, but also their speech is high in their chest. **Imagine a snarling wolf cornered, backed up against a cliff face.** It is a frightened animal with fangs: do you think that what it really needs right now is a hug?

Verbal Control Of Terrified Rage

Your goal here is to reduce the individual's sense of danger. Maintain a safe, distance and relax your posture. Make sure your movements are unhurried, and that your voice is firm, confident and reassuring. If direct eye contact is reassuring for the individual, do so; if intimidating, do not. How will you know? Notice if their body relaxes or tenses in response to your eye contact or its lack. Of course, you should never take your eyes *off* of them: merely that you should not look directly into their eyes if they are terrified by the eye contact.

Initiate a litany of reassuring phrases, speaking slowly, with frequent pauses: "I know you are scared. Put down the book, you don't need to throw that. I keep it safe here. You can put it down now. I'm way over here. Go ahead. Sit down. I keep it safe here."

Do not say, "I'll protect you" or "I won't hurt you." Many individuals who go into terrified rage have been hurt by people who said that kind of phrase. However, when you say "I keep it safe here," you are telling them, "This is my territory and no one, including you, will be hurt on my territory. I am taking responsibility, and because of me, you will be safe."

The individual's body language will also indicate that they are calming down. Their breathing will get a little shuddery or be expressed in short high-pitched gasps. They may slump into a chair or onto the floor as if physically exhausted, even beginning to weep. Tell them to breathe with you, and audibly breathe at just a little slower pace than theirs. You can help them with this by using one of your hands to show the rhythm of your breathing. As they slow their breathing down, slow yours down a little more. Continue to do this until they are breathing calmly.

Figure 14.1 If it is your responsibility to escort a terrified individual

If it is your responsibility to walk the terrified person (who may be a small child) from one place to another or out of an area—if they need your help or it is necessary, for any other reason to go with them, maintain your reassuring litany and slowly approach. If they show signs of again becoming frightened, pause, move back slightly, and continue to speak to them reassuringly.

As you approach the individual, move in **half-steps**: move the right foot a full step, then bring the left foot *up* to the right foot. Pause. Move either right or left foot forward, and then bring the other foot forward *up* to the lead foot. Pause. Because you maintain your legs and feet balanced, with your weight evenly distributed, you can easily move backwards or forwards as needed. Furthermore, because you do not lean forward and 'fall' on the lead leg, as we do when we walk normally, the frightened person does not perceive you as lunging at them. They will be far more likely to tolerate your approach.

CHAPTER 15

Hot Rage

When you think of an individual who is on the edge of violence, hot rage usually comes to mind. Imagine being faced with an individual who is yelling and screaming, brandishing their fists or a weapon, and threatening to harm you. They throw things, tip over desks, and engage in other forms of violent behavior.

General Information About Hot Rage

The more often someone goes into a state of hot rage, the more comfortable they become with it. On subsequent occasions, it becomes easier and easier to be violent. Hot rage is often a tactic that has worked in the past, scaring and intimidating a selected victim either for criminal gain, or just for the fun of it. In a state of rage, such an individual has no concern about longer-term consequences, much less guilt. For some, there is a sense of liberation, even a paradoxical kind of joy when they peak into rage. All one's fears and insecurities disappear, and one is left with only the ecstasy of the pure act. Some people actually desire rage, because that is, to them, the best thing they ever feel.

Displacement is a common factor of hot rage. The individual's anger is displaced, at least temporarily, toward an inanimate object instead of you or another individual. This also includes picking things up and slamming them down, throwing things, punching or kicking walls, furniture, or other nearby objects. However, rather than calming the person down through the mythical 'discharge of tension,' displacement activity escalates them further. Punching a desk or a wall is not what they desire to do—they want to punch your face!

Hot rage is also associated with display, primarily but not exclusively masculine, a primitive attempt to dominate access to objects of desire, eliminate perceived competition, or enhance one's status. Therefore, hot rage can be especially problematic if the individual begins acting out in front of a group of onlookers, coworkers, or family, where to save face, he believes he must act aggressively toward anyone representing authority.

General Verbal Control Of Hot Rage: The Ladder

Figure 15.1 Never Compromise Safety

Do not hold back from any action to keep yourself and others safe if the individual does become violent. Escape, evade, and fight back, if that is what you have to do.

The primary method of verbal control for hot rage is called 'The Ladder.' This is an ideal technique for someone who is beginning to get threatening. It is ONLY used for rage, that gray zone between anger (even extreme anger) and violence. The individual is no longer trying to communicate with you—they are right on the edge of assault.

The technique itself is simple. Identify the most dangerous behavior and repetitively demand that it cease. Use short sentences and easily understood commands. Once they stop that particular dangerous behavior, identify the next problematic behavior and use the same technique. Continue until the individual is no longer aggressive. This technique is only effective right before, during, and after the peak of the crisis because it is a CONTROL tactic rather than a 'lining up' de-escalation tactic. (Remember: control tactics will provoke rage in a merely angry individual, someone we might have over-estimated, due to his/her loud tone, or dramatic behaviors).

As described earlier (Chapter 3), facing an enraged individual causes us to experience fear in a way that anger does not. The danger is NOW, not merely a possibility, were the situation to continue to deteriorate.

What Does Hot Rage Look Like?

Furious individuals are very tense, looking as if they are about to explode. For a mental image, if they are of big stature, think of a grizzly bear; if they are smaller, think of a wolverine. In either case, the image suggests an animal that will tear you to pieces if it perceives danger, if provoked, or if cornered. Furious individuals may display some of the following physical manifestations of their rage:

- Their skin tone is flushed as they become angered, turning red or purplish in color. As they become even more enraged however, their skin blanches, and they turn pale if light skinned, or if dark skinned, they get a grayish tinge.
- Their voice, whether loud or low and quiet, has a menacing and belligerent tone.
- They often pace, inflate their upper body, hit or kick objects, or strike their hands together ominously, punching one fist into the other hand.
- They tend to stare into your eyes directly, or glower from under their brow, with a furious and hostile look on their face.

- Their eyes will appear red or inflamed; usually their eyes are wide open, with tension around the eye sockets and facial muscles.
- Physical arousal, blood pressure, and muscular tension all increase. You may notice veins popping out of their skin, particularly around the neck.
- They may display a smile that shows no humor or joy. Others snarl, or compress their lips with a twist, as if they have a foul taste in their mouth. Still others bare their teeth, or clench their jaws so tightly that the muscles stand out in bunches.
- Once in a hot rage state, they are unconcerned with possible consequences.
- Their breathing is often loud and straining.
- They may claim to be disrespected, humiliated, or shamed. Others will allege that they are not getting their questions answered and their problem solved, or that no one listened or cared. They may rant about 'the system' and claim that they are out of alternatives or solutions.
- At their most dangerous point, they may become calm, breaking off eye-contact, or adopting a thousand-yard stare.

In The Face Of Rage

When confronting a furious individual (and when you cannot escape or get to a safe barricaded position), your posture and tone should be confident, commanding, even imposing. Stand directly in front of the individual, using an angled stance, out of range of an immediate blow. This best prepares you to escape along tangents to his attack, to ward off blows, and if necessary, to fight back. As described earlier (Chapter 7), your hands are either up in a fence, or the wrist of one arm is clasped in the hand of the other in front of you at waist level.

If you stand too close you will appear to be challenging them, too far and you will be seen as fearful: a potential victim. You may have to move forward or backward as needed to maintain this spacing. In either event, move smoothly, without flinching or making any sudden or threatening gestures. When you move with a relaxed body, you are more ready to protect yourself, yet you do not appear as if you are trying to initiate a fight.

Your voice is strong and forceful. Do not shout—instead, keep your voice low- pitched and calm, dropping it into your chest where it resonates; enraged people, in particular, react violently to threatening or angry vocal tones. The only time you would shout is a 'battle cry,' that lion's roar of outrage and strength that you use only when you are trying to stop an actual attack. Maintain direct eye contact, and frequently use their name as you give them commands (see next section).

The Ladder: Establishing A Hierarchy Of Danger

The general hierarchy of dangerous behaviors, from most to least, is as follows:

- Brandishing an object or a weapon in a menacing way. NOTE: If they are too close, or are trying to use the weapon, this is, by definition, violence, not rage. Go for safety! Evade, hide, or fight, depending on what is the best thing to do to help yourself and others survive.
- Approaching or standing too close to you with menacing intent.
- Kicking objects, punching walls, or throwing things (displacement activity).
- Pacing, stomping, and inflating the body in an aggressive manner (posturing).
- Shouting.
- Language that is intended to violate, demean, or degrade.

The Ladder is not merely a verbal intervention. Like any other control tactic with an aggressive individual, you must move as needed to maintain the optimum space to both defend yourself, and exert maximum influence upon the aggressor. If they are very close or threatening, your hands should be up, prepared to ward off any attack, but also as a gesture that is both calming and dominant. On other occasions, particularly when you have more space between you, clasp the wrist of one hand with the other hand.

Give the individual a straightforward command to stop their most dangerous behavior. You are thereby displaying clarity and strength to the aggressor, as well as helping them focus their mind on the most problematic thing they are doing. In a sense, you are imposing order on them. As stated before, your voice should be strong, low and commanding.

After a couple of repetitions, always add, "We'll talk about it when you ..." followed by the same command. Once that behavior is stopped, pick the next most problematic behavior (the next 'rung' of the ladder), and command/require that it stops. If the aggressor does calm down and stops all the aggressive behaviors, including assaultive language, THEN set a firm and direct limit.

This is not the time to try and think of something brilliant or life changing to say. By keeping things simple, you can continue to look for escape routes, identify potential weapons, and attempt to get help. If you know their name, intersperse your sentences with it frequently, using this to pace and break the rhythm of your commands, as well as trying to re-establish a human interaction.

Continue working your way down the rungs until the individual is no longer in a state of fury. If the individual re-escalates to a higher and more dangerous activity, simply return to that rung of the ladder and begin again. Remember to stand and use your voice as described in the previous sections.

The last 'rung' is probably swearing or other obscene language. Remember, some individuals swear as punctuation, without any hostile intent. They may be crude, but they are not trying to be verbally violent. *For example, "I'm sorry, I was just mad at my f**king daughter, and s**t, you happened to arrive at just the wrong damn moment."* If that kind of language offends you, it is something you should deal with at another time. However, <u>if the swearing is an attempt to violate you, it must be dealt with in proper order</u>. Do not focus on the language, no matter how vile, if the person is **doing** something dangerous. Remember aggressors will use language to shock, distract, immobilize or terrorize you—their behavior is far more dangerous than anything they are saying.

When you use the Ladder, one of three things will happen:
1. They keep on coming; you will do what you have to do to ensure **safety**.
2. They get close and when you tell them to step back, they say, 'make me;' you will do what you have to do to ensure **safety**.
3. They comply. When individuals in hot rage comply with the command to step back, they usually do so yelling and screaming, "you can't tell me what to do!" Others, who are displaying their power for others, strut back, as if it was their choice (they are 'saving face').

Once you have them fully compliant, having followed your directives, you must still maintain control. Only after setting very strong limits could you shift into problem-solving, even with a family member. Otherwise, they will assume that the best way to get a reward, your attention, or help is to abuse you.

Figure 15.2   Example: The Ladder

Your voice is firm, low pitched and commanding, as you 'descend' down the rungs. In the following scenario, each statement is, of course, in response to something the aggressor has done or said. Do not talk too fast. Although these phrases in the text seem to follow one-after-another, do this with a <u>slow, controlled pace</u>. Pause between each phrase. Use command presence, not hysteria!

- "Step back. Step back. Robert. We'll talk about it when you step back. Robert. Step back. Step back, Robert. We will talk about it when you step back."
- "Stop kicking things. Robert. Stop kicking things. We'll talk about it when you stop kicking things."
- "Robert, I cannot follow you when you pace around. Sit down and we can talk. Sit down, Robert."

Notice the paradoxical message, that you cannot 'follow' them. Of course you could, if you wanted to. You are trying to catch their attention as they try to make sense of what you said. We want them thinking again, trying to figure out what you said and why you said it. We want the part of the brain that thinks things through taking over from the part that is driving them towards violence.

Imagine, however, that they have stepped forward again, thus ascending to a higher "rung" on the ladder.

- "Step back! Robert! Step back and we'll talk. We will TALK about it when you step back, Robert. Step - - - - -back."
- "Sit down Robert. We will talk about it when you sit down. I cannot follow you when you are walking around. We will talk about it when you sit down."
- "Lower your voice. I cannot hear you when you yell that loud. Lower you voice and we will talk."

Here is a second paradoxical communication: of course, you can hear an aggressor who is shouting loudly. Once again, you are trying to create a 'glitch' where he tries to figure out what you mean when you say you cannot hear him when he is yelling.

- "Talk to me with the same respect that I talk to you. We will talk about it when you stop swearing. Stop swearing. Robert. We will talk when you talk to me with respect, the same way I talk to you."

Don't forget, people often swear as punctuation. They have no hostile intent whatsoever. If the individual is swearing in this manner, it is not a problem. However, if the swearing is an attempt to violate you, it <u>must</u> be dealt with in proper order. <u>However, do not focus on the language, no matter how vile, if the aggressor is doing something dangerous</u>. Remember that predatory individuals will use language to shock, distract, immobilize or terrorize. What they are doing is far more dangerous than anything they are saying.

CHAPTER 16

Cool (Predatory) Rage

Thankfully, this type of aggressor is rather rare. They are intimidators. The predatory individual may deliver threats in cool, dangerous tones, often *after* a clear and strongly stated demand. Then they offer you a chance to avoid injury if you comply. A variant tactic is to *pretend* being out of control. This is in contrast to a genuine attack, an action that they may also be eminently capable of and willing to carry out. My symbol for them is either a leopard or a shark, depending on if they present as 'warm-blooded' or 'stone cold.'

While these individuals seethe with hostility and/or contempt for others, they have developed these emotions as a deliberate weapon of terror, perhaps even enjoyment. Paradoxically, their physical arousal is often low. Their heart rate can actually go down and they can be charming and engaging, even as they prepare to commit an act of violence. This disconnect between appearances and intentions can cause you to lower your guard, because you may have a hard time believing that someone whom you believed to be a seemingly nice guy is willing to terrorize you psychologically, or hurt you physically.

They actually have no inhibitions regarding their aggression other than tactical calculation or self-interest. They have no capacity for sympathy or guilt, and many experience low levels of anxiety in situations that would frighten ordinary people. Every time they successfully intimidate someone, their behavior is reinforced. They view inaction on your part, either during the confrontation or afterward, as either weakness or tacit approval, thereby increasing the likelihood of similar behavior in the future.

The best response is a combination of power and dispassion. The former is obvious. Strive to never be in a situation where you are vulnerable with such an individual (Do not worry—I will discuss what to do when you are not in the more powerful position in subsequent sections). By dispassion, I mean that you, as much as possible, do not make it 'personal.' Do the best you can so they do not 'get to you.'

I am aware that this section may seem way too abstract, and therefore, make these people even more frightening. So, let's make it clear in the following sections—what, specifically, should we do and say when facing a cool, predatory individual?

Principles: What to Do When You Do Not Have Overwhelming Force

Your basic task is to demonstrate that you are not prey, and that the individual's attempts at intimidation will simply not work. Most predatory individuals do not wish to interact with someone whom they *cannot* intimidate or otherwise control through emotional abuse or physical posturing. Instead, they seek more subservient victims, where their chances of success are greater. When engaging a predatory individual, you should remember the following:

- Stand or sit ready to move. Be poised, but do not appear fearful or too defensive.
- Avoid gesturing or expressive movements. Fear often causes

your movements to be awkward, and the aggressor will see this as confirmation of their control over you.

- Be open and strategic about everything you do: the way you position your body, your voice, and your posture. The predatory individual is well-versed in reading body language and assessing weakness. Don't pretend anything. Protect yourself openly, and do not change your actions based on what they say, including their efforts to put you at ease or promises of compliance.

- Another tactic the predator may use in these circumstances is to use anything you do against you, either deriding you or pretending that you are out of control, paranoid, or acting strangely. Ignore all that, and openly act to keep yourself safe.

- Do not make explicit or unrealistic threats, such as: "If you come near my family, I will kill you!" That tells the predator what you will NOT do. In his mind, if you really meant it, you would do it now. An explicit threat is an empty threat.

- Do not over-react to vague threats. The predatory aggressor will interpret your reaction as a victory. If, however, the individual makes an explicit threat to harm you, then this is a police matter (after you have removed yourself from the situation safely).

Cryptic Consequences: To Extricate Yourself When You Do Not Have Overwhelming Force

Keep your voice matter-of-fact, and give clear and direct statements of *potential* consequences. If you can, smile. These consequences are of a special type: clear, but cryptic. For example: "You know what would happen if you did hit me." In this case, do not tell him what would happen. Let his imagination take over. These vague consequences are a mirror of his/her own method of intimidation, and he/she may likely react to you as 'not prey, not edible, not worth the trouble.'

If he/she says, "What are you talking about?" you should reply, "You know exactly what we are talking about." When the predator responds to your cryptic consequence with questions or with confusing statements that would make your statement illogical, simply say, "You know what is going on here. You know what is happening." You may have to intersperse your vague consequences with ladder commands if he/she escalates his/her behaviors.

Try to minimize eye contact. However, you need to look directly at him/her, so look between the eyes, or look at him/her with a flat stare, as if you are looking at his outline. Your eyes are flat as buttons, with no attempt to 'penetrate' or make contact; you should make sustained eye-contact only if in a fight for your life. Then, you must shift focus, trying to penetrate his/her eyes as if you were a laser beam. (NOTE: in Figure 16.2 below, I will outline a complete sequence of interaction between a predatory individual and a person protecting himself/herself from them).

Figure 16.1 Cryptic Consequences: A Tool Rarely Used

You ONLY use cryptic consequences with the openly predatory, that most rare of people, and ONLY when they are escalating into predatory rage, <u>and only when you do not have sufficient force or backup to otherwise control them</u>. In other words, it will probably never happen happen, but you need to know what to do if it does. NOTE: In case you think this is a tactic for some tough guy or hero, two weeks after I presented at a community college, the sixty-six year old dean of students called me up. She very happily described an incident where a six foot, nine inch out-of-work logger, who was flunking out of nursing school (because he hadn't done any of the work), threatened to come back on campus with a chain saw and start cutting people down like trees. In a voice that sounded exactly like Julia Childs, she described using cryptic consequences successfully. He left her office, she immediately called law enforcement and he was arrested before he left the campus.

This is, therefore, NOT a tactic for some kind of action hero—it is a tactic for ordinary people like you and me, who simply demonstrate to the predator that we are 'too much work.' In other words, all we are demonstrating is that we are not easy prey.

Responding To Explicit Threats

Do not over-react to his/her threats, or he/she will interpret your reaction as a victory. Certainly, if you and your family have been threatened (whether the tone is velvet or harsh), you must do everything necessary to keep everyone safe (Appendix I). You may have to be on your guard for a long time, and you may need the help of law enforcement to do so. That said, the first task is getting away from them right now—and this strategy is geared to make the predator leave. Imagine a cat about to grab a bird, and the latter, to the cat's surprise, suddenly pecks her right in the nose. The cat retreats to wait for a better opportunity.

Figure 16.2 Example of a cryptic interaction with predatory individual

"Look, this is very simple. I think you and I can agree that you misinterpreted what I said about hitting my child. I don't know where you got the idea that I said I beat her. I said I spanked her, a little swat so she wouldn't run into the street. Look, I understand. You must have been having a bad day, and you over-reacted. This can be fixed very easily. Just call the police and tell them that you didn't quote me accurately, that you've been overworked lately and misjudged the situation. See, I bet you love your family as much as I do. You've got your child in a good school over at Echo Lake. Actually, it's amazing, that's one of the last schools in this area that still lets the kids out for recess. It's nice to see little kids playing so happily and innocently.

Oh, sorry, I'm a little off track. What I'm saying is that I bet you would be devastated if anything happened to your family. I'm the same. The problem here is that what is happening to my family is you! And this is a problem you could fix, unless you are really sitting there telling me that you want to destroy my life and that of my child. IS THAT WHAT YOU ARE SAYING??!!!!"

You. (*With a little smile and a strong, confident voice*) "I'm really glad we're having this conversation, because it's good that we both understand each other."

Predator. "So you'll make the call."

You. "Oh, you know what's going to happen."

Predator. "Suppose you tell me."

You. "There's no need to do that. You know exactly what's going on."

Predator. *(Getting a little confused)* "Are you threatening me?"

You. "I don't know where you got that idea. In fact, we both know the situation here."

Predator. *(Walking away after a hard stare)* "You think this is over. You better watch your back."

Please note that this exchange could conceivably go on for a longer period of time. I am here presenting enough back-and-forth that you should clearly understand the principle.

SECTION V

Intense Styles And
Difficult People

CHAPTER 17

Dealing With
Difficult People

Some people have a style that makes them really difficult to communicate with, particularly when there are problems. They may be co-workers, family members or anyone else with whom you come into contact. However, most of our problems in this area are with people whom we know. What will help in dealing with them is:

- The ability to recognize the behavior as showing a pattern.
- Knowledge of best practice communication strategies to respond to a person who is displaying the pattern, whatever the cause of the behavior may be.

The goal of this section is simple, whether you regularly encounter such individuals or not—we will be at our best when we prepare for the worst.

CHAPTER 18

Coping With
Stubborn Refusals

There are many occasions when, despite having treated a person with clarity and respect, they refuse to comply with your requests, or let an issue drop. Of course, if you have been bossing them around, patronizing them, or treating them with disrespect, it will not be surprising if they resist you. All people have pride, and no one likes another person talking down to them or controlling their life.

If you are clear that it is not your approach that is creating the problem, what, if anything, can you do to elicit compliance? You will find the following steps helpful:

- **Focus on the task.** Never take an individual's non-compliance personally. This just adds additional problems to your relationship with them.
- **Clarify the message.** You must be clear on what the person is requested to do. Do not bring up previous examples of their non-compliance, such as "the last time this happened," or "you always," or "remember when you...." Stay very specific.
- **Control the interaction.** Stay on topic and do not allow the person to divert your attention to unrelated issues.
- **Use a strong and calm voice.** Keep your tone of voice strong, but not demanding or aggressive.
- **State the consequences.** In certain cases, you should be very clear in explaining to the individual the consequences that may be imposed for non-compliance. This should be provided as

information, rather than threat. For example: "Unless I receive the requisition, I will not go ahead with the shipment." Or, "If you don't pick up after yourself, I will no longer cook for you." This is done in the same way you inform a child on a cold winter day, "If you stick your tongue on that metal pole, you are going to get stuck."

- **Place the power in the individual's hands.** Without handing over one iota of your authority, allow the individual to be the decision-maker, and clarify their role in complying, or not complying. Don't threaten the individual—simply state the facts of the consequences for non-compliance. In a sense, this could be thought of as a 'low-key ultimatum.' Perhaps say something along the lines of:

  - "It looks like you've got something to decide. You are absolutely correct. You don't have to do it. You can discuss matters with your union. Or, we can sit here, treating each other with respect and try to figure out a solution."

  - "Martin. You are welcome to live here. You either will pick up your clothes, clear your dishes, and all the other chores that you know are your responsibility here—that you NEVER need to be reminded of again, because you do know what they are—and in that case, I will cook meals for you as I have. But if you do not fully participate as a part of this family, and fulfill ALL the responsibilities that are yours, you are welcome to make your own meals."

CHAPTER 19

Dealing With
Mood Swings

Individuals with mood swings can be verbally abusive, provocative, complaining, passive-aggressive, blaming, apologetic, ingratiating, and friendly all in the space of an hour, or less. They can be very difficult to communicate with, much less de-escalate, because just as you make progress with their current mood, they shift into another. They often try to get control of us even when they have no control over themselves.

Coping With Mood Swings

Rather than respond to the individual's specific mood with body language or words that manifest your own anger or frustration, remain balanced and emotionally non-reactive. *You influence them by being exactly what they are not.* The more you are unaffected by their emotional storms, the more likely the individual will calm down

- Do not mirror the individual's emotional state
- Control them through controlling your own emotions. Remain powerfully calm.
- Speak in a firm, yet calm and controlled manner.
- Don't dump too much upon them! When swept by intense emotion, it is hard to think. They may want to work things out, but if you talk too fast, too elaborately or with too many ideas, they will feel confused. This will make them angry, because it is YOU, with all your words, who is making it so difficult. <u>If you pace things slowly enough, they may have time to think things through.</u>

CHAPTER 20

Stuck On
Grievances

Some individuals store up grievances, allowing feelings of persecution and perceived personal slights to affect their entire worldview. Frequent complaints about old history can become a significant source of conflict, not to mention being extremely aggravating.

You must refrain from reacting emotionally to the individual's inability to move beyond the past, even as you try to redirect their attention to the present situation. Above all, do not personalize the individual's complaints or their feelings of prior injustices because you will get stuck in their world of grievances:

- **Acknowledge their concerns.** Quite often individuals merely need to express their frustrations or feelings of helplessness regarding their situation, and they view you, at this moment, as the only available outlet to do so. As long as they do so in a non-aggressive manner, there is no problem. Do not agree or disagree with them, or otherwise reinforce their feelings of persecution, just recognize their complaints and then move forward, in a 'once and done' manner. If they raise the issue again in subsequent encounter, emphasize that you have heard these complaints—you can quickly paraphrase what they are upset about to prove it—and refocus them on the issue of current concern.

- **Apologize.** When an individual complains, yet again, about something directly concerning you, think about it very carefully. Perhaps, in this instance, you were wrong. If so, apologize sincerely and fully. In some situations, this is enough. However, I cannot stress strongly enough that you should be wary of apologizing to an individual simply to mollify them. Such an apology may lead the individual to believe they are now in control of the relationship—that you are intimidated and will try not to upset them in the future.

- **What if an apology is not enough?** You might say to the individual, "You are still upset about this. You want to talk about it again, don't you?" Notice that you don't ask the individual: you merely state what you understand. This gives them the opportunity to correct or adjust your understanding, so that if their complaint turns out to be legitimate, you are able to effectively put it to rest.

- **Complaints as their own reward.** Certain individuals are never satisfied, because the complaint becomes a 'rewarding' activity in itself. Others bear a pervasive resentment toward you, an institution, or even life itself. For them, complaints are merely a way to express hostility or an attempt to control communication by getting you to talk about things on their agenda. In these cases, simply take the issue off the table, forever. Remind them that you have already addressed this complaint, so that there is nothing more to discuss. If necessary, terminate the conversation. If they bring it up again in further encounters, firmly state that you two have: already solved this issue, you have already apologized, or you have said all that can be said. You then go on to say that, therefore, there is nothing more to talk about concerning this situation.

CHAPTER 21

Responding To People In
Disorganized States

Will You Ever Need To Calm Or De-Escalate Someone Who Is Disorganized?

Disorganization is any mental state where an individual struggles with thinking and feeling, so much so that their ability to communicate and/or process information breaks down. This sounds like a really extreme position, but how many of you are responsible for the care of an elderly loved one who may be suffering some level of age-related decline, perhaps dementia? How many have cared for—or work with—someone who is developmentally disabled? How many of you have ever responded to a lost and frightened child? How many of you have ever had to deal with someone who is intoxicated on drugs, alcohol or suffering from a medical emergency that affects their cognitive abilities?

If an individual is in a disorganized state, they may be impulsive, and when really confused or overwhelmed, potentially striking out in all directions. The most salient characteristic of disorganization is the near impossibility of establishing *any* lines of communication with people experiencing it. They may utter cascades of words that seem to make little sense, or even grunts, moans, and mumblings. Others make sentences based on rhymes, puns, or cross-meanings, their brains capriciously linking words together based on sounds, not meanings. They may speak in repetitive loops, fixating on one subject. They may laugh or babble, completely at variance to the seriousness of the situation.

Disorganized people can easily become quite frightened or irritable, especially if they are overwhelmed with stimuli, such as a large number of onlookers.

How To Communicate With Someone In A Disorganized State

Only one person should be talking to the person. Use calm movements, and a firm but reassuring voice. Chaotic individuals often experience poor motor control, vertigo, disorientation, etc. Slow movements and soothing tones of voice help orient them physically and emotionally (NOTE: By 'soothing, I do not mean 'soft and sweet.' I mean calm, low pitched and powerful). Use simple, concrete commands, because complex sentences or detailed instructions will be confusing or threatening to the individual. Disorganized people are *sometimes* susceptible to distraction by being deflected to another topic. In this case, you can sometimes start talking about something that catches their attention. One powerful form of distraction is to offer them food or drink, or in some cases, place a loved object in their hands (as long as it can't be used as a weapon). With frightened, disorganized children, I have sung to them.

One of the last things we retain is our name, so use their name, repetitively, interspersing it frequently in your commands in order to get their attention before initiating attempts to redirect them to another activity. Be very cautious about touching disorganized people, as this may be experienced as invasive, or even as an attack. Particularly with children or a confused elderly person who may do something that will put themselves (or others) at risk, you may need to physically guide them to a safer place, but be prepared that they may try to strike, hit, kick or bite you (think of an enraged toddler).

Use simple, concrete commands with no more than a single 'subject' in each sentence. Repetition several times is almost always helpful. Use only one thought at a time, as complex sentences will be confusing, and thus threatening or irritating. For example, say slowly, "Sit down, William. Sit down. Sit down. William, sit down." Or in other circumstances, "You're safe here, Mrs. Summers. You're safe here. You're safe here." Or, in other circumstances, "I love you, poppa. I love you. I love you. Now lie down. Yes, lie down. Lie down right here. Lie down."

Minimize such distracting behaviors on your part as extraneous body movements. Your movements should be calming and also only be those useful in helping the person understand what is going on.

Figure 21   A Powerful, Calming Presence

Because of their difficulty in attending to what you say, non-verbal communication is the most important aspect of your communication. A calm reassuring presence, manifesting both strength and assurance is your best hope of helping to stabilize an individual who is in a disorganized state.

CHAPTER 22

If There Is A Problem Here, That Is Your Fault: Useful Tactics for Dealing With Paranoia and Claims of Persecution

Figure 22   Paranoid Character Traits

This chapter focuses on tactics specific to an attitude, with the following characteristics: a sense of being persecuted, blame of others for any problem, and a hair-trigger sensitivity to being vulnerable. This is a character trait that is actually rather common, and always difficult. This chapter is not about *delusional paranoid* people, for example, someone suffering from schizophrenia or drug psychosis. Nonetheless, the principles in this chapter do apply to communication with someone in such an extreme state.

The paranoid individual's motto of life could be summed up in a phrase: "If there is a problem here, that is your fault." The paranoid world is one of winning and losing—the paranoid person tries to dominate the other people in his/her life. Such people can cause all sorts of problems, due to their consistent attitude of blame, resentment and defiance of authority, hypersensitivity to criticism, fear of vulnerability, denial of responsibility for any problems that might occur, and belief that others are out to get them.

Paranoid people are, underneath, terrified that they will be made vulnerable, but they are aggressive toward that which they fear. One help-

ful image of the paranoid person is an
angry porcupine, all quills, with a soft
underbelly, hunched over, ready to
strike in hair-trigger reaction.

Paranoid people interpret relax-
ation as vulnerability. Therefore, they become more paranoid when
you begin to establish rapport with them—if you 'get' them to relax,
they believe you'll catch them off guard and take advantage of them
(For this reason, paranoid people are particularly volatile within their
families). Because friendship means letting your guard down, do not
be surprised if paranoid individuals suddenly flare up with suspicion or
accusations during times that are uneventful or even friendly.

Being mistaken or wrong is another form of vulnerability. Rather than
admitting wrongdoing or mistakes, paranoid individuals reflexively
project negative feelings on the other person. If they feel hate, they
believe, "You hate me." If they forgot to go to an appointment, they
will claim, "You set me up. You knew I couldn't get there on that day."

Paranoid people live like detectives, searching for evidence to prove
what they already know is true. They assume that others are conspiring
about them, talking about them, or laughing at them. Ironically, their
actions, in response to their paranoid ideas, frequently cause others to
act in exactly the way paranoid people expect.

Because of their aggressive or standoffish behavior, they can make other people uncomfortable or afraid. If they sense fear in you, however,
they expect you to attack, because that is what they do and they 'attack
you back first,' feeling fully justified because they *knew* "what you were
about to do."

Try To Let Them Know What Is Going On

Because paranoid individuals are so suspicious, they will often question your actions and instructions. It is especially important with these individuals to clearly and explicitly explain the situation you are involved in, particularly if you are in a position of authority. By the way, if in a position of authority, you should always **front-load** potential consequences of violation of company policy and non–compliance with rules. In other words, make the rules absolutely explicit when anyone enters your organization. If you make the mistake of soft-pedaling rules to create a 'welcoming' atmosphere, the paranoid person, in particular, will feel blindsided if you later inform them of a rule when they commit an infraction.

Dealing With The Paranoid Individual

- **Maintain the angle.** Whether standing or sitting, turn your body at a slight angle, so that physical 'confrontation' is a choice rather than a requirement. If you directly face a paranoid individual, they feel controlled because you 'force' them to turn away if they don't want to face you.
- **Mindfulness.** Never let down your guard. You are in an avalanche zone, and however peaceful it's been for the last six months, anything could set off another slide.
- **Too friendly is as dangerous as a threat.** Try to be aware when things are getting too comfortable. If the paranoid person relaxes, they may suddenly startle, realizing that for a brief moment, they let their guard down. They may respond with aggression to make sure you do not 'take them over.'
- **Differentiate.** Paranoid individuals feel safest when you differentiate yourself from them. It is better to be somewhat emotionally reserved rather than too warm and friendly.
- **Cover your buttons.** Paranoid people will try to provoke you. If you lose your temper, they will feel justified in whatever they do to you as well as it keying into their terror-based ag-

gression. A slang expression for this is 'fear biters.' They bark and snarl and when you react, they attack as if you had gone after them first.

- **Correct Distance.** Given what I have already written, it is clear that the ordinary ways we try to establish respectful and decent relationships don't really work with people who assume the paranoid stance. Rather than warmth, understanding and empathic approach, the best way to relate to the prickly, hypersensitive person is correct distance. Be a little formal. Be matter-of-fact. When you communicate, keep your body upright, but relaxed. Do not try to ingratiate yourself. Rather, deal with situations as they occur—with dispatch and clarity. Imagine trying to relate to a porcupine—hugging it is not a good idea, is it. Instead, do the opposite.

CHAPTER 23

The Volatile Personality

Volatile people believe that whatever feeling they are having right now is the only possible reality. Those on the mild end of the spectrum will be quite emotional, over-reacting to things that others could take in stride, displaying frequent mood swings (Chapter 19). For those who are more severe, it is as if their nervous system, at least that part which regulates emotion, seems to lack any protective sheathing. Imagine trying to live your daily life with two layers of skin peeled off. Their current emotions are inescapable. They experience the world and the people in it as good or bad, perfect or foul.

Dealing With The Volatile Personality

Volatile individuals are, not surprisingly, quite reactive to *other* people's emotional reactions. Therefore, the most important component to calming such people is staying calm yourself. Throughout this book, I discuss specific tactics on calming down angry and enraged individuals—those strategies are universal. Beyond that, we must assume a particular attitude with volatile people, particularly those who are members of your family or workspace; your attitude should be similar to a perfect uncle or aunt, someone who wishes the individual well, yet undeviatingly expects certain behaviors. I refer to this as 'warm non-attachment.' You are most likely to get into a dangerous situation with such individuals when you ramp up your emotions in reaction to theirs. It is much like dealing with a three year old in an adult body. Surely you can keep calm when dealing with a toddler having a tantrum! This is really no different: it's just that because their body is larger, they are more dangerous, and because we expect better of them, we get offended when they are so emotionally volatile and abusive. Control yourself and your reactions and you will have the best chance of controlling such people when they get out of control.

CHAPTER 24

Bad Intentions:
Recognizing The Strategies
Of Predatory Individuals

In order to satisfy their need for instant gratification, some individuals attempt to manipulate nearly everyone with whom they come into contact, including family members, strangers on the street, and fellow employees. Some use manipulation as a means of furthering criminal actions. Some view us as opportunities to gain something they want or animated toys to play with for their own amusement. Others live for hate and destruction, but delight most in duping people so that they do not even know how 'dirty they were done.' Some predatory people lie so well and often that no one can pin them down, using a 'divide and disappear' strategy so that the more powerful beings in their life argue about them, instead of focusing directly on what they are really doing. (NOTE: at the extreme, very rare level, these individuals display Predatory Rage – Chapter 16).

Strategies

Manipulative strategies can result from a variety of emotions and intentions, such as those born of revenge, malice, desperation, laziness, guilt, or as the result of drug and alcohol use. In some situations, you should also be wary of individuals who appear to be overly eager to please. Their seemingly compliant behavior may in fact be nothing more than an attempt to manipulate and control you. Often their dishonesty is the result of '**lies of omission**.' For example, such an individual perceives your caution at entering the meeting room and he/she says:

- "You can come in. The walls are all glass. Everyone can see inside."
- "I guess you are a little uncomfortable meeting with me today, because I had trouble with my last teacher. You don't have to worry—that was personal. It had nothing to do with you."

Neither of these statements establishes, in the slightest, that he/she does not mean to assault you.

Another sign of coercion is a **reassuring promise when none was asked for**. For example, you are walking back to your car from a restaurant and an individual approaches you. "Mr. Carcetti, I know you might be concerned about me approaching you, you not being on the clock and all. That's why I came up, because if you saw me and I didn't say hello, you'd think I was up to something shady. Are those your kids?"

Predatory people sometimes use stories, overloading you with **too much information** to keep your attention away from what they are doing, either in your presence, or more generally, in the worksite. They charm you so that you actually look forward to meeting with them, but remain unaware of what's really going on.

Predatory individuals will also ask you for **personal information**, such as marital status, children, in which part of town you live, and so forth. These questions seem to be innocent enough, just the normal back and forth of a pleasant conversation. What the predatory individual is doing, however, is gathering information, something that they can use later in the relationship. You should be careful about answering any personal questions, particularly when your intuition is signaling you that something isn't right (being polite should never trump being safe!).

Predatory individuals are also **quite adept at behavioral observations**, such as noting the body language of others. They are particularly interested in potential victims, those who are easily intimidated or frightened, as well as someone putting up a front, pretending to be tougher than they are.

Manipulative individuals are also likely to **blame others** for both their failures and their behaviors. Nothing is ever their fault: they were simply in the wrong place at the wrong time; they did not know their friend left the marijuana in the company car; it is the your fault that the police or their probation officer is coming down so heavily on them.

The predatory person **plays one person off against another**—they deliberately agitate people on the worksite whenever possible, through gossip, initiation of conflict, or provocative actions.

Predatory individuals also view their **relationships as transactions** with an eye towards gaining an advantage or placing the other individual in their debt, perhaps by doing them a minor favor.

Just as a leopard or a cougar is known to attack whenever a vulnerable animal turns its back and exposes its neck, predatory individuals **feed off vulnerability**. They study everyone with whom they come into contact, making note of any apparent weaknesses and developing new strategies of manipulation and control. **Not only do they lack a sense of remorse at the harm inflicted upon their victims, they often take uncommon delight in it.** Do not assume, by the way, that I am merely talking about a criminal. This may be the lawyer who is working with your union or the executive assistant or vice-president who should be doing his/her job.

Once you realize that an individual is behaving in a manipulative or predatory manner, your goal must be the protection of the people in your family or worksite. Your personal and professional integrity is paramount as you have a lot to lose, including your reputation, your career, and your personal wellbeing, if you succumb to the predatory individual's attempts to manipulate and control you.

Tactical And Safety Considerations

The following will be helpful in your dealings with individuals who exhibit manipulative and predatory traits:

- **You will be attacked through your best *and* your worst points.** The notion that the manipulative individual will attack your weak points seems quite logical. If you are insecure about your personal appearance, for example, the manipulator will either make you feel more insecure, or in a more sophisticated tactic, reassure you that he/she, at least, finds you quite attractive. What is harder to notice is when you are attacked through your best points. For example, if you appear to be physically fit, they will try to consult with you about your exercise regimen or ask where and when you work out. If you go to church, they will find a way to ask a very intelligent question about an aspect of the Bible you love so much. But they are asking you to gain some traction, not to get your help. For such an individual, anything can be leverage. Remember, they do not even have to lie. The truth is an even better tool. (Example of using the truth as a strategy: They confide in you about their sick child, but they are not really asking for help. They know that they can elicit your sympathy and in that process, may let them get away with things you otherwise wouldn't allow).

- **Notice when others start making excuses for the individual.** When conned or manipulated, people often find a way to rationalize what the predatory person is doing or has done. For example, after a frighteningly angry outburst at your church, in which the police escorted him off the premises, a pastor says, "You have to understand. He was brought up that way. When you told him he had to leave the Sunday school classroom, it was like a flashback to the way his father treated him." Do not permit others, no matter what their professional position, to sway your opinion or prevent you from attending to your safety.

- **Track any manipulation, note it well, and alert everyone in your circle what strategies they are using.** Do not discount the observations of others. Ensure everyone shares a common understanding of what and whom you are dealing with.
- **You may be intimidated.** The most obvious manifestation of intimidation is fear. <u>There is always a reason for fear</u>. If you are frightened of an individual, consult with others, including, in some cases, the police. What is more difficult to recognize is an unconscious attempt to avoid being frightened by colluding with their behavior, or giving into their demands. Ironically, the intimidated person may sometimes claim that they have a special rapport or working relationship with the individual, when in fact, all they are doing is giving the predatory individual what he/she wants.
- **Be aware of grooming behaviors.** The 'grooming cycle' is a pattern of behavior designed to alleviate the intended victim's fears and apprehensions, while targeting them for attack. The individual will make their target feel a little off-balance, making them anxious, scared, or flattered. Then they lessen the pressure while making a request that you would have granted anyway. The manipulative person begins to 'train' you to experience a sense of relief when granting a request.
- **Do not get beyond the horizon line.** *Do not meet predatory people alone!* For example, do not close your office door when interviewing them—you are vulnerable to false accusations. You are also vulnerable to manipulation, because with no one to monitor the interaction, you may not even perceive it happening; and of course, you are vulnerable to attack.

SECTION VI

Communication
With Aggressive
Young People

CHAPTER 25

What Has Happened
To Our Young?

Despite all the material blessings of our modern society, many young people are having a very difficult time. Ostracism, for example, was once the equivalent of a death sentence – in earlier times, cut off from one's family and tribe, one had nothing left to do but die. And children are ostracized all the time.

Bullying makes one tough, some people say, and yes, it is true that to grow up strong, on occasion, you have to stand up for yourself. Yet how can a child stand up to *systematic* bullying—where a much stronger person or even a group makes a single child the object of sadistic torment that goes on and on and on? The child is also trapped by a youth culture that condemns the child who 'snitches' far more than the bullies. And often, if they do stand up for themselves, fighting back in self-defense, their school treats them as equally at fault, violating their sense of equity and fairness.

A couple of generations ago, parents mulled over how to introduce the topic of sexuality—and the timid might leave their child a book on their pillow that explained in some detail what happens between a man and a woman with a note, saying, "If you have any questions, just ask." Kids used to look up 'intercourse' and 'sex' in the dictionary, and check, just to be sure, that 'f---k' was not there as well. Today, he or she googles 'sex' and gets tens of millions of hits, with films of transgressive and obscene acts, some of which, truly, never existed before a combination of drugs, money, desperation, and degenerate imagination enables filmmakers to coerce people into doing just about anything. With the Internet the normative touchstone of youth culture, many children and teens end up coerced or attracted to sexual behavior far too young, far too uncaring of their partners, and/or skewed far from the norms of ordinary human sexuality. Please understand that I am well aware that the panoply of people's sexual fantasies and activities is not confined to a single norm, but do your own browser search: you will find that something has gone terribly wrong when our children's sexual education informs them that sex, as often than not, seems to involve extreme acts that border on torture and push well over the line in terms of contempt and degradation of everyone involved, but particularly women.

Drugs are everywhere, and not only do they affect children directly; far too many have been affected *in utero* by their parents' drug use. Furthermore, when one's parents regularly drink and do drugs, their attentiveness and caring toward their children are lessened in the 'best' of such circumstances—abuse of all kinds increases exponentially in drug/alcohol abusing homes.

Gangs metastasize within a community like a cancer. There is a putrescent vitality to gang life that is both charismatic and compelling. Despite the terrible things they may do, the gang offers solidarity, and a life committed to something bigger than oneself, however damaging that life might be. Once initiated, one crosses a line over which it is hard to return. This charisma, by the way, is not only attractive to children from broken or abusive homes—the vitality of a warrior culture, no matter how violent and destructive to both its victims and its own members—seduces children from loving families as well. It is only when 'the good' has a power and charisma greater than that of gang culture that youth find it easy to turn away.

We live in a culture that bombards us all not only with images of sex, but also of impossible, romantic love—that without a relationship, one's life is empty. Furthermore, we all will be lovable, if only we smell right, look right, walk right, dress right, think right, perform right, talk right, are shaped right, and are sure to drink the right beer when standing near a woman in a bar. The major preoccupation of many teens— no, pre-teens, even children—is whether one is in a relationship, is doing what he or she has to do to keep the relationship, or what to do now that one has lost the relationship. School, rather than a place of learning, is, for many, an enclosed environment in which a preoccupation with who likes whom achieves cosmic importance. Many kids are defined as useless material for a relationship, both by themselves and by their peers. Others squander much of their waking hours obsessing over their looks, their weight, and all the rest of the artifices that, applied correctly, might make one worth spending time with.

Enough? One could write an Ecclesiastes, a dirge for the lost innocence of our children. Suicide? Violence? Why not? Both are a problem-solving activities, when you cannot think of another viable solution to the problem that traps you. Do many of our children find themselves so trapped? Beyond counting.

CHAPTER 26

Are Aggressive Kids
Any Different From
Aggressive Adults?

Generally speaking, you can use the same de-escalation strategies with youth as are outlined in the rest of this book. The differences are often more on nuance than on major details. I have, however, 'subdivided' young people into some general categories based on behaviors that will help both in understanding them as well as using the best strategies to help stabilize and calm them when they have become aggressive or are otherwise in crisis.[3]

One significant additional factor we must consider is the particular dynamic that exists between teenagers and adults in Western society. Modern Western culture is unique in our 'creation' of teenagers as a special class. In most societies, one was a child until one became an adult, through some transition or initiation, usually connected to one's functional ability to procreate and/or fight. Such young adults might have been viewed as having a lot to learn and they would have been quite low in a social hierarchy regarding their elders or family, but they were still expected to fulfill an adult's responsibilities.

---

3   I am indebted to John Holttum, MD, Child Psychiatrist from Tacoma, Washington. I attended a presentation given by Dr. Holttum that influenced me greatly in terms of how to 'subdivide' the behaviors of aggressive youth and how best to intervene with them. I must underscore that any intervention recommendations are mine, and may be at variance to those Dr. Holttum might offer.

These days, due to the requirements necessary to educate someone, emotionally and intellectually, for a mature role in our far more complex society, the assumption of adult responsibilities is quite delayed compared to other cultures—including America and Europe of a century ago.

Because we have deprived our children of something they desperately need—responsibility (work, chores, maintenance of the home, helping to raise children, etc), they have a lot of freedom. With financial support from their families, they have become commercial targets. There is a multi-billion dollar industry that focuses all its attention on how to please young people. In traditional cultures, youth idolized adults, because with adulthood came both responsibility and privilege. The creation of a commoditized youth culture has reversed this—far too many adults envy youth, trying to dress and be like them. This is made worse by the fatuous 'cult of self-esteem,' where a child is praised for existing, not for any accomplishment. All of this causes many young people to affect an arrogant stance—they assume that they are eye-to-eye, equal with their elders. They speak to adults as if they are peers, or even inferiors, and sad to say, far too many adults agree.

When children emerge into modern teenage society, they are not *primarily* concerned with either maturity or integrity as an adult, or security and happiness at home as a child. They desire to stretch their wings and feel powerful. They measure power by their effect on others, particularly their peers. Consider then, if youths view adults to be their peers, they will be preoccupied with who is more powerful and will vest considerable energy in not being powerless in relationship to them. To make matters all the more difficult for everyone, power, too, has been commoditized. It has been made synonymous with violence. Many teens will naturally see intimidation (which can be everything from violence at the extreme end to such subtle gambits as the 'silent treatment,' where a teenager makes an adult anxious and over-eager to reach them) as means towards achieving a powerful role in this world.

What so many teens tragically lack are 'true adults' – individuals who do not believe that power is merely a dynamic between predators and sheep, that there is a power of humanity that does not resolve itself around violence or terror, but is manifested by integrity and dignity. Because there is, among all our drives and desires, this deep innate passion to mature, even among very volatile and troubled youth, such true adults will have charisma. These adults will draw kids to them without any apparent effort. Their attitude is not, "How can I please or reach you?" Instead, it is a simple invitation: "Here I am. You are welcome here. But I don't need you here either. It's up to you."

Because so many aggressive youth use negative attention as the means to engage adults, you must have a spacious-enough attitude and spirit to powerfully respond to dangerous behaviors without over-reacting. Teenagers, especially, experience fear and rage as being out of control. At the same time, they'd like to believe that through aggression, they can *take* control. Every time you can deal firmly and effectively with an angry teenager without losing your temper, you demonstrate a kind of power that is at variance to loss of control, but very attractive to teens who may have never seen it before. This is contained power, power expressed with dignity and grace.

CHAPTER 27

No Brake Pads—
A Consideration Of The
Impulsive Youth

We have an alleged epidemic of Attention Deficit Disorder (ADD)/Attention Deficit Hyperactivity Disorder (ADHD). Per orthodox theory, attention disorders come in two major forms. In the first type, the main manifestation is a short attention span. In the second type, hyperactivity is also present. I must note that the diagnosis of ADD/ADHD, now so astoundingly common, deserves more controversy than it is currently receiving in both media and clinical sources. I strongly recommend that everyone concerned with youth read two contrarian books, one by Leonard Sax and the other by Richard Louv.[4]

Whether you end up agreeing with all of what Sax or Louv proposes, each requires you to think afresh about these issues. And in an era where medications are slung like bonbons at children, often with little clinical assessment or sound treatment, this is absolutely necessary.

Let us here consider the impulsive child who, whatever diagnosis is or is not applied to him or her, tends to act before he or she thinks.

---

4   *LAST CHILD IN THE WOODS:* Saving Our Children from Nature-Deficit Disorder by Richard Louv (Algonquin Books [a division of Workman Press], Chapel Hill, NC, 2005), and *BOYS ADRIFT:* The Five Factors Driving the Growing Epidemic of Unmotivated Boys and Underachieving Young Men by Leonard Sax (Basic Books [a division of Perseus Books] Philadelphia, PA, 2007).

- He is in a store and sees a video game he wants, and without considering the consequences, shoplifts it right in front of the security camera.
- She gets in an argument with one of her friends, and in front of an entire classroom, blurts out the secret that the other girl entrusted her.
- Another boy bumps him in the hall and he stabs him in the hand with his pencil—he is as surprised as the victim, both of them looking at the bloody pencil tip with their mouths open in shock.

Coupled with a degree of difficulty in deriving satisfaction by methodical step-by-step work, impulsive youth often engage in disruptive or thrill-seeking behaviors. Aside from any interventions, from educational plans to cognitive therapy to medication, impulsive youth need an activity that consumes their interest. They are able to focus with remarkable attention when they are doing something about which they can say, "This is me." This activity gives purpose and meaning to their lives, a touchstone they—and you—can use to help them organize those more difficult situations where they do not feel at home.

The impulsive young person gets angry or aggressive for the same reasons as any other person, but they get particularly upset when they get frustrated or when someone interferes with the gratification of an impulse. Once swept up by this anger, it is hard for them to stop. Tactical Paraphrasing (see Chapter 11) is particularly valuable, as you validate their desire and their frustration rather than argue with them about it. If, however, they are too escalated for paraphrasing, it is not the time for explanations, attempts to elicit sympathy for the other person or moral preachments.

What is often best is a calm demeanor and simple short commands that the young person do exactly what you tell them to do. Your demeanor is calm and authoritative, with the attitude that defiance is inconceivable.

Figure 27 Are Impulsive Kids Really Ill?

A woman described her childhood in a radio interview. She could never keep still in her seat at school, was disinterested in most academic activities, was disruptive with her playmates, and defiant with her teachers. Her desperate mother took her to a psychiatrist who sat the two of them down, and ignored the child and talked about her and about other things for a good half hour. The child stirred in her chair, picked things up of his desk and had to be told to put them back, hummed to herself, played with her hair, and any number of other disruptive etceteras.

Then the psychiatrist told the mother he wanted to talk with her in another room, told the child to wait, and as he left, pushed a button on a recorder. As they walked out, the room filled with music. He closed the door, and told the woman, "Watch." Through the glass, they saw the child swaying in her chair, moving her arms, and then she stood and began to dance.

The doctor said, "She's not ill. She's just in the wrong place. This child needs to dance. Take her out of school and find her a place."

The woman grew up to be a famous ballerina with the Royal Ballet.

Before you default to the medical model, and particularly the medication model, consider if your child is simply in an environment that puts him/her at the mercy of his/her impulses—because s/he belongs somewhere else.

There are countless, immensely talented kids, and there are others ready to do something simple but well, who were not born to succeed in the cookie-cutter, often violent, poorly run, union-dominated, common-core driven public school system. Get them somewhere better for them, and their 'disorder' will disappear—or no longer be such a major problem.

CHAPTER 28

Fierce Youth

Fierce youth are often startling to us because they seem to be without conscience or caring for most other children or adults. And sometimes, they truly do not care. They may display rages in two categories previously described: hot rage and cool predatory rage (Section IV). The fierce character can develop from a myriad of reasons, some of them heart-rending. This may be relevant if they are in therapy, or if they are a family member and it is your responsibility to try to undo a horrible past, but it is not relevant to the de-escalation and control of their anger or violence. Particularly with these fierce young people, someone will be seriously hurt if you contextualize or excuse their behavior.

Attempting to establish a sympathetic or nurturing connection with an aggressive young person is often a mistake, particularly during a rage state, and this is **particularly** true with such fierce youth. They experience these gestures as an attempt to soften their defenses, and/or as a sign of weakness on your part. In other words, sympathy is experienced as manipulation or an attack. Fierce youth lay extreme importance on protecting themselves from 'invasion.' Therefore, any loss of control, which is implicit in a softened response, is viewed as weakness.

They strive to defend themselves against any emotional need or attachments with others by building up a callous attitude. In the most basic way, fierce youth are profoundly isolated—they have very limited human ties. All they have is an inflated and easily bruised sense of pride, their most important 'possession,' something for which they will live and die. This pride, however, can be an access route for communication and de-escalation. <u>The formula for communication with such fierce youth is "**respect outweighs sympathy.**"</u>

In other words, enforce rules with calm gravity and strength. Never try to ingratiate yourself, as this will invite contempt. Trying to 'prove' that you care will have a negative effect. If you manifest yourself as a strong and dignified adult who does not make it 'personal' when you give advice or set limits, you will, sometimes, draw their attention and curiosity. He or she may possibly begin to question: "How come she has nothing to prove? Why, even though she isn't frightening or even trying to frighten me, is she not weak? Why isn't she, like so many others, sucking up to me, trying to please me?" If there is hope for such youth, it lies in their fascination with power. **You present to them a world unimaginable, one where power and human decency can exist within the same body.** If you do not behave in this manner yourself, such a fierce young person will be unreachable.

Figure 28 Are Fierce Youth All Sociopaths?

Considering the ferocity of some such youths, it is easy to default that they are irredeemable—perhaps born evil. I spent a year in a youth detention facility—a 'kids' jail—teaching physical stress reduction techniques derived from Chinese martial arts. Young men cycled in-and-out of my classes as they went to court and dealt with their misdemeanors, or in some cases, were sent to long-term youth detention facilities. There was one young man, seventeen, who showed up at my class for many months. He was a very handsome boy, tall and graceful. He talked with none of the others.

I asked about him and was warned, "Be very careful with him. He was tried for attempted murder as an adult, and they are just waiting for a place for him in the youth wing of the state prison. When he ages out of that, he's got a long sentence ahead of him. Anyway, don't turn your back on him—he beat the man almost to death."

Week after week, he did the exercises diligently, and unlike most of the other boys, never joked around, nor was he ever disruptive. One day I was told that he was being moved that afternoon—this was his last class. As he walked past me, I said, "I hear you are going up today." He merely nodded, and walked on. He went through all the postures of the exercises—dynamic stretches, really.

The class ended, and the other twenty or so youth walked out of the common area back to their cells. The young man, uncharacteristically, lingered. He walked right towards me, staring, and I waited. I did not know if he was about to attack me—he reminded me of a cougar: graceful, beautiful, and unreadable. About five feet away, he veered off to the side and walked past me. Over his shoulder, he said, "I wish you were my dad."

Had this happened earlier, I would have assumed that he was trying to play me, to manipulate my sentiment or appeal to my ego. That he said it when we both knew he would never see me again, proved that he meant it. I do not mean he was in prison unjustly, nor that he was no longer dangerous. Truth be told, in certain circumstances, he would have been dangerous to me. But he wanted to let me know that he saw what I offered—and furthermore, he let me know that he recognized what this meant; young men need adult males who truly care for them and treat them with respect.

My point here is that if he could recognize what he had missed in his own life, he was not irredeemable. As are, I would underscore, most such fierce young men and women.

CHAPTER 29

Dynamite Under A Rock—
Explosive Kids

Many of these young people can pay attention just fine. Others, such as a child with Fetal Alcohol Spectrum Disorders or a history of head injuries, cannot. Their hallmark quality, however, is that once their fiery temper is unleashed, it is very hard for them or anyone else to stop the emotion. They rage and rage and rage and rage. They are the kids, of whom one says, "Billy lost it again today," and everyone nods, imagining the slung chairs, the house trashed, and possibly the one-half hour physical restraint that followed.

Orders or other firm commands do not work well with these young people. They can be appallingly violent, and they react to commands as further provocation. The watchword, instead, is **containment**. You may have to give commands, but your voice must be very firm and calm. The command is to get their attention, to focus everything on one being: YOU. In favorable circumstances you, and however many other people (family, people at your place of work, etc.) are necessary, in a matter-of-fact, deadpan way, escort this young person to a quiet area where they calm down on their own. Your task is to stay nearby so that they do not injure themselves or damage property. You cannot, however, problem solve or otherwise work things out while they are still on fire. If you are unable to accomplish getting them to a quiet place where they can be contained or where they can contain themselves, you should avail yourself of the strategies on rage and violence (Section IV).

Figure 29   Children with neurological deficits

Some such explosive youth, particularly those with neurological damage, will also suddenly shift into an 'organic rage,' apparently unmediated by cognitive processes. However, these kids often show small micro-changes of behavior right before assaults. With youth with whom you have an ongoing relationship, you should definitely do what you can to learn these signs to help them shift gears into another activity or process, thereby heading off the explosion. This is something you should raise with the youth's treatment professionals as well.

- A girl in a group home had enacted a number of apparently sudden severe attacks against other residents. We found that when she focused on an intellectual task too long, she would begin scratching at her forearm. The 'sudden' explosion of aggression followed a few minutes after this 'tell.' Therefore, as soon as she scratched her arm, she was redirected into another activity.

- Another youth would knit his brows and glower in a stubborn manner when he didn't understand a conversation. He interpreted this as people "making me feel stupid," an attack, in his view. This facial expression was a clear sign to slow down, lighten up, or change the subject.

CHAPTER 30

"You Can't Make Me, And Even If You Do, I'll Still Make You Miserable" —Argumentative Youth

There is a particular term used in psychology for kids who argue about everything, even when it is against their best interests or even their own desires: Oppositional-Defiant Disorder (ODD). Many clinicians consider this to be a genuine diagnosis, a behavioral disorder of childhood. Others (myself among them) reply that it is disordered behavior, but that it is an artifact of a dysfunctional culture, be it their own family or their neighborhood and friendships. This reflexive defiance of authority, particularly that of those most familiar (parents, teachers), usually develops in homes typified by poor boundaries (too dictatorial, too invasive, too lax or too chaotic).

Their aggression is typically against 'family'—those familiar to the child.
- Dictatorial parents, who try to break the child, often 'create' defiant kids among those who are too strong-willed to crumble. The motto of such kids seems to be, "You will not break me. Furthermore, even if you make me do it, I still say 'no."
- Other parents who are not consistent or do not enforce coherent reasonable discipline (overly permissive or chaotic) also elicit such behaviors. In this case, the child is implicitly saying, "I will act out until you are forced to give me some limits."
- In still other cases, the parents have not raised their children poorly, but the kids have perniciously bonded with other

young people or with an image that they absorbed from some media, either of which encourages defiant behavior.

- Finally, exacerbated by drug or alcohol abuse, many hitherto loving young people turn nasty indeed.[5]

Negative reinforcement—only giving attention for negative behavior—will elicit more negative behaviors. Reinforcement through punishment that is both out of proportion or inconsistent teaches the child that discipline is an attack, that the parent is unpredictable, and that acting out at least gets the parent's focus on them. The child experienced a kind of 'social power' when punished. They see the punisher as having the right to define good and bad, but at the same time, they see themselves as having impact (if they are not utterly broken in spirit or body by the punishment).

Sadly, once power is acquired in this manner, the child gets a grandiose sense of his or her own importance. Frustrating and defying adults becomes its own corrupt reward.

Sometimes these kids are surpassingly argumentative, fighting over fine-points, while claiming to not be understood. They apparently thrive on conflict—they look for any pretext to continue the argument and knock you off center. This is often not a search for truth or equity—it is simply a power tactic. The truth is that they hold in contempt adults who take this overly seriously. <u>If you are losing your temper, they are winning</u>. It is important for the adult, perceiving this tactic, to disengage and not participate in fruitless badinage or argumentation.

Perhaps the most important recommendation I can make is that all people involved with argumentative youth must **maintain consistent**

---

5   The most important book discussing these issues is that of the author, Leonard Sax, cited previously. This book is called: **The Collapse of Parenting: How We Hurt Our Kids When We Treat Them Like Grown-Ups,** Basic Books; Reprint edition (May 9, 2017)

rules with NO deviations. The argumentative youth will test these boundaries over and over again to see if the rules have changed.

Pick your battles. Do not waste energy arguing about anything that is not important. When it is important, you must become implacable, like a huge boulder slowly, inexorably rolling down a two degree slope. They put energy in their argument—you put the weight of granite in yours. You are an adult. **Do not argue with such a youth as an 'equal'** – instead, you tell them what will be, with no negotiation whatsoever. If you are correct in what you require, it should be experienced as a force like gravity – not a debate.

Figure 30

I once worked with the parents of a young girl, fourteen, who was so argumentative, so defiant, that she was sneaking boys into her room to have sex, even though she derived no enjoyment from it. She sold herself out to have power over her parents, making them both anguished and helpless. They had already sent her to five different therapists, to no avail. In fact, things just got worse.

Over six weeks, I worked with her very nice parents, so nice that neither of them had set any limits on their daughter whatsoever. They hated what their family had become and what they were becoming in the process. We set up a system of rules, of consequences, of a family system that was as predictable as the solar system—there was a lot of space for each planet to shine, but each was required to follow a defined orbit. (NOTE: I refused to meet the daughter; that had already been tried. Rather, I coached the parents).

The parents were adamant with their rules and at six weeks, the girl escalated, pushing her mother into a wall. The mother countered the push with one of her own, pinning her daughter against the wall herself, and told her, "You will go to your room. You sit and consider that you just used violence against the woman who gave you life, just because you are not allowed to do something that is not good for you anyway. And when you have thought about it, you owe this home 'community service.' You will clean the living room."

Some hours later, the father returned and found his daughter on her hands and knees, polishing the wooden floor (this was not the task). Surprised, and knowing nothing of the incident, he said, "Thank you." And she replied, "I didn't do it for you, daddy. I did it for me."

There is nothing wrong in a child's drive for power. It is our responsibility that we guide our children in power that includes respect, decency and cooperation. Understand, this young woman hated herself for what she was doing—but somehow she couldn't see another way to feel powerful. It was the job of her parents to show her that – and ironically, in this instance, she found it on her hands-and-knees, polishing the floor.

CHAPTER 31

Pseudo-Nihilism—
I Don't Care

As odd as this may seem, such a youth, who asserts that his or her life is pointless or boring, as well as enacting self-destructive behaviors, is striving for power. By making themselves outcasts, they are inviolate vis-à-vis the larger society and its goals. Their sense of power increases when they can horrify, disgust, or offend others. Taken further, they achieve power when they experience themselves as unreachable by other people.

You should not be emotionally bland with such youth. Instead, you pay attention to what the young person presents and offer them a human reaction. If you try to show that their provocative behaviors do not affect you, they will escalate until they do evoke a reaction. ("Oh, you didn't react when I scratched my wrist? How do you like this necklace of burn scars around my neck?").

If you do succeed in 'stonewalling' them, all you have succeeded in doing is establishing that you truly don't care—and that is different from an all-too-convincing pose of uncaring.

On the other hand, do not over-react. It is *their* problem, not yours, as hard as this may be to believe, particularly if they are a family member. Beyond a 'human reaction,' what you must, in fact, show them is that you are inviolate—their distress, their frightening or repulsive behavior will not control you. You demonstrate that you don't *need* them to change, and that you are, in your own way, free—in fact, far freer than they are. One of the most striking things about rebellious youth is how they clump with others assuming the same fashion. Your ability to be unique embodies what they profess they desire.

One is most concerned about youth of this type by what they hide inside. These kids, in particular, need an adult to be a 'fair witness' to their world, able to provide feedback in a way that he or she does not feel compelled to resist. They need someone with more life experience to talk with.

Figure 31 Moon in Still Water

I once met with a young man—sullen, seventeen, dressed in a Goth style, with a history of minor assaults, and what everyone concerned with him described as social alienation. He actually had friends much like himself. He used some drugs, and had damaged his skin in some rather creative ways with fire and blade. We met in a coffee shop. For forty minutes, he made no eye contact, and merely stared off in space. So after buying him a coffee, I was silent as well. Finally, I said to him: "Given that your dad is paying for this, I can be here all day. But honestly, I'm getting bored. Before I leave, I'd like to throw something out here—I've met your dad and I'm a very different man than he is. In fact, I would not be surprised if I'm different from anyone you've met. I don't mean better—just different. So if you want to run something by a different man you may never see again, here's your chance."

After some silence, he asked me a question on how to handle it if his former girlfriend started going out with his *former* best friend, if it was OK to beat him up. I pointed out that with his size and age, he'd probably be arrested as an adult, and "Even though your friend broke the 'code,' there's no girl on the planet worth going to prison over." He stared into space a bit longer and left. Over a two years span, I talked with him twice, in similar fashion, at his request. Then, no contact at all. I wondered what might have happened to him. Five years after that, I got an invitation to his graduation at an Ivy League school, and a note: "You were a big part of me being here."

Without patting myself on back, let me analyze what this means. He knew that somewhere, whenever he wanted, there was a man available to speak about whatever he wanted, someone who didn't need him to be anything. With that 'breathing space,' he knew the experience of being who he knew himself to be.

The pseudo-nihilistic stance is an act of 'defensive war' – in essence, with all 'your' (parents, society, media) influence, I cannot see clearly who I am. I will, therefore, repel you so I might have a chance.

Unfortunately the repellent stance brings its own baggage, including self-hate, so clarity is usually not a part of the experience. You, my readers, can provide that—although if the youth is someone you love, this is incredibly hard. You want to tell them they are special, you want to slap them upside the head and tell them to get a grip, you want to weep with them over what is causing such alienation. But if you can be the equivalent of a calm lake where they can sit nearby, you offer them the best chance of emerging from this alienated, lonely stance into a life of integrity.

SECTION VII

It's Not Enough
To Do The Right Thing—
We Must Be The Right Thing

CHAPTER 32

Training Your Intuition
To Pick Up Danger

Intuitions are sometimes vague, but they are often the first signs that a dangerous situation is developing.

- Never minimize your gut feelings and intuitions when informing someone else of your concerns. Do not begin by stating "I know it's nothing, but…." In doing so, you may lead others to minimize the situation as well. For example: Imagine you see signs that the person your son or daughter is dating resembles an abusive person in your past. The signs are subtle. You consult with another family member, but because you have minimized the situation, the person you are consulting with takes your lead and 'agrees' to discount your intuitions. Later, you are proven right and your child is hurt.

- Do not be hesitant because you or others do not have 'hard evidence' to support your concern(s).

- Sometimes one person in your group (or family), often someone who *claims* to have the most experience, may belittle others' intuitions of danger. Differences among you must be discussed respectfully, particularly in regard to questions of safety. In many circumstances, each person has only part of the picture. If one person's idea or intuition is discounted or dismissed out of hand, he/she may cease to speak up, and vital information regarding everyone's security will be lost.

Shapeshifting: How To Assess Your Personal Space

A sense of spatial awareness, of potential escape routes, likely weapons, and access to help should become a natural part of your life. This routine attentiveness is often referred to as 'having street smarts.' This comes naturally to some people, but not to others. The core of this is to gain insight into the thinking patterns of aggressive people were they to enter your territory or when you enter theirs.

Awareness of escape routes, potential weapons, and access to getting help should be as natural to you as to an antelope that surveys a valley for predators before entering open space. Your considerations must go beyond practical questions such as what objects you will place on your desk and where you decide to put your chair, be it a workspace, or how to arrange the articles within your home. Use a tactic called 'shapeshifting' to get insight into the intentions and type of planning that potentially aggressive individuals have:

- Enter a room with a predator's mind and a predator's movements: slowly, gracefully, with calculation. Imagine that you are going to hurt the next person who comes in that room. How would you cut off their escape routes? What could you use as a weapon? Where would you position yourself to attack? Where could your victim best escape?

- Moving in the same manner as a predator or other aggressor (or any of the other aggressive styles described elsewhere in this book) enhances your ability see the world through their eyes. If you are in the habit of noting potential danger (items that can be thrown, sharp objects, etc.), you will have a greater likelihood of avoiding harm when it is offered.

- Do this on a regular basis. Consider it a refresher course on the mind of an aggressor or predator. Done over time, you will start to develop the ability to automatically scan any room to see if there is anything there which makes it a place of danger, as well as switching your mind on to picking up predatory or other dangerous behaviors on the part of individuals.

- I am well aware that many of my readers are not accustomed to seeing the world this way. I think what you will be surprised, even shocked, to find out is how easy it is to shift into this mindset. If you are human, you have the capacity for aggression and violence. Therefore, if you decide to view an environment with a predator's mind, you will find, perhaps contrary to your expectations, that you are very good at it. As shocking as this may be, the upside is that you therefore have the knowledge to anticipate how real predators think and therefore, will be able to prepare for them.

Figure 32   Intuition Saves Lives

In my capacity as a mental health professional, I was requested to visit the rented home of a woman whose behavior had changed in a troubling way. This was the kind of job I had done innumerable times. I approached the house and was just about to knock on the door when something indefinable, almost a physical command, told me to back away, to not touch that door. I did just that, returned to the clinic and wrote in my notes that the home should not be approached without the support of law enforcement. One of my co-workers, a woman, instead of regarding me as overly nervous, heeded my advice and during a subsequent visit, accompanied by police, found a very distraught woman, psychotic, a previous victim of terrible violence, armed with a pistol. Because of her previous experience—sexual violence at the hands of men—she only trusted two types of people: women in general and the police who had previously rescued her. She willingly gave the gun to the law enforcement officers and accompanied my co-worker to the hospital.

However, on that previous day, had I, a stranger, a man, knocked on her door instead of obeying my intuition, I have no doubt whatsoever that she would have opened the door and shot me.

CHAPTER 33

The Texture Of Relationship—
Intuition In Action

Communicating with hostile individuals is often difficult, particularly when they become agitated or angry. You must develop the ability to differentiate between actions that bear the very real possibility of physical attack, as opposed to a person simply trying to express their frustration or venting about their personal problems.

While there is no surefire method of predicting an impending attack, the description of aggressive behaviors elsewhere in this book will enable you to better predict the likelihood of the individual escalating to physical aggression. Beyond that kind of concrete data, this chapter will focus on developing your ability to **sense** when a potential aggressor is beginning to escalate.

Comfort Zones And Physical Spacing

The leading edge of intuition is a sense of personal space. This is not a mere matter of feet and inches—simply asserting that you keep an arm's length and a half, or two arms lengths between you and a hostile person is not enough. How much space would you want if the person has a blade, is twice your size, or half your age?

Our mood can also affect our sense of space. For example, the more relaxed you are in the company of someone you trust, the less personal space you require (unfortunately, we must remain aware that this is something that manipulative or predatory individuals take advantage of). When you are uncertain or suspicious of someone, you instinctively move to get more distance from them. If you are having a bad day, you need more space to tolerate anyone's proximity. In short, the presence of other people elicits physical and emotional reactions when they are impinging upon your space.

Figure 33.1 Two Cautions Concerning Personal Space when interacting with someone who is hostile or otherwise potentially dangerous

- DO NOT knowingly step inside someone's personal space, unless doing so makes you safer.
- DO NOT accommodate anyone by allowing them to stand within your 'bubble,' the space where you are comfortable interacting with that person.

You MUST be aware of the physical sensations of someone in your 'zone.' When you set such a limit as "Sir, I very much wish to hear what you have to say, but you are standing too close to me. Move back and then we will continue to talk." (Please note that the formal tone is deliberate in this example, appropriate to dealing with someone on the worksite). The reply you get will be great threat assessment information. You are dealing with very different individuals when one, told to step back, responds with profuse apologies compared to someone who smirks and says, "What's the matter, are you nervous around men?"

The Brain Wants To Survive

There are parts of the brain that are primarily focused on survival of the human organism itself: they do not care about being polite, politically correct, or intellectualizing why someone might be aggressive towards you. These parts of the brain do not use words. They perceive by recognizing significant patterns. The portions of the brain that focus on survival are fast, about half a second faster than the thinking brain. If you are about to step on a squiggly shape on the ground, the adrenaline hits and you jerk back your foot even before the rest of your brain thinks, "SNAKE!" <u>Instead, the signal is through physical sensations and emotional reactions.</u>

You can train and develop your intuition. We do this through becoming more aware of the signals our bodies send us. Paradoxically, many of us get 'skilled' at tuning out those signals, treating them as a kind of unwanted 'noise,' particularly when it concerns other people. We don't want to be rude, we don't want to misinterpret, be judgmental or prejudiced, we don't want to cause a scene and so we learn to suppress the signals the 'survival brain' sends us, often to our detriment.

If someone is aggressive, psychotic, excited, depressed, menacing, hateful, or is trying to con you—any 'strong' interaction—the survival brain recognizes a pattern in what they are doing, and reacts. For example, when in proximity to a frightened person, perhaps you feel warmth in your chest, but with a con-man, your lips compress and neck tightens. With individuals suffering from overt mental illness, and you feel a sensation of cold in your stomach and your hands and jaw clench with aggressive people. There are no rules to these physical reactions: they are individual to you. Another individual would experience different physical reactions to the same person. However, your personal reactions tend to repeat in recognizable patterns. Just as you can learn to recognize when your child had a bad day at school based on his or her behavior, you can reliably recognize both patterns of behavior on the part of the other person and patterns of reaction within yourself that very quickly give you warning of another's intentions.

Some of your physical reactions may be unpleasant or unflattering to your own self-image. For example, let us imagine that you get somewhat sick to your stomach when facing an aggressive person, or experience a subtle, but real sense of revulsion when dealing with someone who is depressed. You do NOT need to change this reaction. When you are a person of integrity, your feelings and emotions convey information, but they do not *demand* that you act. For example, let us say that you are talking with a relative and you notice that previously mentioned sense of revulsion. Rather than ignoring or suppressing it, you take it as a signal rather than a value judgment. Although he is smiling, perhaps talking fast, you know that this physical sensation happens to you very often when dealing with despairing individuals, and he was, many years ago, so down that he made a suicide attempt. So you shift the conversation to determine if he is depressed. You know that a sense of hopelessness and helplessness, the hallmarks of that state of mind, have led him in the past to thoughts of suicide.

If you continue to hone your awareness in this matter, you will develop a form of conscious intuition called **MINDFULNESS**. Mindfulness is the ability to be consciously aware of what is going on in your interactions with another person.

Figure 33.2 Honing Intuition

It is very easy to train yourself to become more intuitive. Carry a small notebook in your pocket. If you encounter an individual who interacts with you in a significant way (aggressive, manipulative, depressed, etc.), note down (later) how your body reacts.

IMPORTANT NOTE: We should be far more concerned with physical sensations than what we normally refer to as 'feelings,' our description of emotional states. For example, you have a sensation of high energy, with tension in your stomach. Some would call this 'anxiety,' while others would call this 'anticipation.' If you think that a sense of anxiety does not 'fit' the situation you are in, you will tend to ignore the physical sensation. If, on the other hand, you merely associate a physical sensation with a situation, for example, "Every time someone tries to con me, I get a little smile and tension in my neck." You will notice your physical reactions without biasing them based on what you think you <u>should</u> feel.

Where these reactions really come in handy is when someone is trying to hide their intentions: smiling, for example, while trying to get close to you to hurt you in some way. Let's say, in this case, it is a disabled woman in your neighborhood whom you helped when her baby choked on food. Your 'thinking mind' tells you, "She wouldn't want to hurt me! I saved her baby's life!" But your eyes are tightening and you are getting the same tension in your lower back that you have had on every occasion when someone has attacked you in the past, either verbally or physically. Don't talk yourself out of it! Danger – and a very sharp point - is about to hit you right in the gut. ***By taking notes on sensations, you are training yourself to CONSCIOUSLY RECOGNIZE the patterns that your survival brain notices on a subconscious level.***

Figure 33.3 Ignoring Intuition

I had a close friend. We shared a common interest, training in martial arts. He'd travel many hours to train with me, sometimes staying overnight at my house. We had lots of fun. However, increasingly, I began to have a very unsettling physical reaction, not only when he was around, but also when I thought of him. I brushed it off – he was my friend, we trained together in somewhat dangerous techniques, and he had proven, time and time again that he was trustworthy on the mat. He practiced 'clean.' Yet the physical sensation of disquiet would not leave me. I discounted it, giving myself every explanation other than the one that should have been associated with that sensation, at least based on past experience – simply put, "This guy intends you harm."

Eventually, I learned that he was trying to damage my reputation. I could have saved myself several years of this unpleasant subliminal stress had I acted on the warning right away.

It was as if I had a smoke detector, and I covered it up. It was still picking up the subtle smoke of this slow burning fire. I could 'hear' the buzz of the signal. But instead of paying attention, for all too long, I simply covered it up with another 'layer of denial.'

CHAPTER 34

It Is Not Personal
Unless You Make It So

Do not personalize any disagreements if you intend to avoid getting sucked into stupid or dangerous arguments. What usually happens, though, is that we believe ourselves justified when counter-attacking, because they 'hurt us first.' Responding to an aggressive individual on a personal or emotional level will cloud your judgment, while distracting you from legitimate safety concerns.

Some people use obscenity and verbal violation to get you focused on what they are saying rather than what they are doing. Others suddenly perceive in your response to what they said that you have lost your composure and they 'attack you first,' because they believe you are about to attack them in response to what they said. Others challenge you by *trying* to offend you or by making you explain yourself. Provocative challenges are for the purpose of getting leverage on you.

At any rate, although their attacks on you might *seem* personal, that is only true if you make them so. If the attack is untrue, what is there to be upset about? And if what the individual said is valid, you knew it anyway, so what are you upset about?
- They call you fat? Well, you knew that already, didn't you?
- They called you a Nazi? Well, you aren't, so why are you taking it personally?

No One Will Own Me

The verbal aggressor is trying to 'push your buttons,' often in an attempt to elicit an off-centered reaction. As previously described, the brain is organized to respond to danger through pattern-recognition. A large object moving rapidly towards us, a sudden pain, or a violent grab initiates a cascade of responses—fight/flight/ freeze/faint/flinch—that are geared to keep us alive in the worst of circumstances. At lower levels of danger, particularly that presented by another human being, we are provoked into posturing—dominance/submission displays—that serves to maintain or enhance our position in a social structure.

The curse of being human, however, is that these survival responses are precipitated by any noxious stimuli, particularly those that shock or surprise us. When someone unexpectedly violates our sense of right and wrong or verbally assaults us, we often respond by automatically shifting into those primitive responses, even when survival is not truly an issue. ***When our buttons are pushed, we react as if we are threatened with bodily harm.***

Bracketing: Naming Your Hot Buttons

Anything that puts you off-balance puts you at risk. Therefore, it is important that you are aware of what your buttons are. Use a technique called ***bracketing*** to make it harder if not impossible for others to even get to your buttons. Bracketing is a technique that entails facing your vulnerabilities head on, so that no one can use them against you.

Here's a worksheet that can help you name and bracket your own hot buttons. (You can make a photocopy to work on it separately from the book). Some example statements may include:

- I can't stand it when someone attacks or demeans < >, because that's something I love and treasure.
- I feel outraged when someone demeans < > because it is something I believe to be unquestionably right and good.

174

- People get me defensive when they say or point out < >, because, to tell the truth, I hate it in myself . . . or, (it is a personal flaw and I know it).
- When people say or do < >, I lose it because it's as if they are taking control of me, or disrespecting me.
- They better not say < >. That's the one word I won't take from anyone.

Statement	Why does this get to me?
EXAMPLE: When people say or do < >, I lose it because it's as if they are taking control of me, or disrespecting me.	

34.1 Hot Buttons or Triggers?

There is a new cultural meme, one that is hurting rather than helping people deal with verbal aggression: 'hot buttons' are now referred to as 'triggers.' This is an unfortunate trend. A button is like a wall switch: tripped at the wrong time, it can cause a blinding flash of light, but we can flip that switch off again. A trigger is what arms a bomb or fires a gun. You cannot un-fire it. As I discussed earlier (Chapter 3), people who believe themselves to be 'triggered,' (and it is a belief, not a fact) feel helpless and unable to suppress or control their extreme emotions: fear, anxiety or rage. They are unable to see a situation in context. They become emotionally flooded if they hear a certain word, for example, no matter what the intent of the other person. Once upset or angered, the 'triggered' individual justifies whatever they do *because* they have been 'triggered.' The irony is that this is exactly the same justification that aggressors use for their violent acts.

It is a moral responsibility to master oneself. Whatever your profession or station in life, you must develop yourself so that you respond to crisis or aggression by becoming the 'eye of the hurricane'— you compel the chaos to revolve around your calm center. We all have buttons—I certainly do—but the art of living one's life with integrity and dignity is to roll with the punches, be they emotional or physical: not counter-attack or crumple because we allow ourselves to become emotionally off-center. We cannot *differentiate* what type of aggression a person is manifesting—or if they are, in fact, aggressive at all—if we do not have mastery over our emotional reactions. We can control and master 'buttons,' but once we are 'triggered,' we no longer have either control or moral agency.

Using The Information From Bracketing

Not surprisingly, we are most likely to lose our temper when we are blind-sided. Sudden emotional shock elicits the same responses in the nervous system as a physical attack.

To avoid this, you must do the equivalent of looking both ways before crossing the street. **Every morning, upon waking, and maybe even a few times during the day, simply run an inventory, as if flipping through a set of cards, and call to mind each of your hot buttons.** By bringing them to consciousness, you prepare yourself for the possibility that someone may try to set you off that day. Some people might find this sort of inventory depressing, but this is no more valid than complaining about being required to check your mirrors before backing out of your driveway. When an aggressor tries to push one of your buttons, you are not surprised or caught off guard. You expect it without being anxious about it. If you take inventory, you center yourself for another day, ready for the worst without it tearing you down.

Figure 34.2 The Power of Bracketing

A Security Professional of my acquaintance is of Samoan ancestry. He encountered an extremely irate customer, who came into the building, demanding to speak to the CEO. As he attempted to help him and calm him down, the man began calling him a variety of racist insults. The Security Professional, who had practiced bracketing to specifically deal with his protective pride regarding his heritage kept his cool, and was able to calm the man down, and actually provide the help he was seeking (without him getting to see the CEO, of course, which would have been a 'reward' for his aggression).

CHAPTER 35

The Joy And Intoxication
Of Righteous Anger

Most people consider anger to be a harmful emotion, one that upsets the angry person as well as the recipient. This is not true for everyone. There is a subset of people who do not mind fighting whatsoever, particularly when they believe their cause is just—and they are not necessarily 'bad' people, either! These individuals go off-center in an interesting way, becoming calm, even happy, when someone offends them. As a boxer once stated in regards to an opponent, "When he gets hurt, he wants the round to be over. When I get hurt, I get happy."

Such people have an especially difficult task. **They must recognize that when they feel good, they are in danger of becoming part of the problem**. Instead of imposing calm, they escalate the situation, not minding it in the least.

Circular breathing (Chapter 36), for those who are anxious, stressed, or frightened provides a real sense of peace and relief. However, if confrontation feels good to you, such calm breathing seems like the last thing you would like to do. You think, "Center myself? Hell, no. I'm right where I want to be."

If this description fits, your task is to recognize the special joy that comes with righteous anger, and act to center yourself to a calm state of mind, even though in the heat of the moment, it feels like a loss rather than a gain.

If this is you, recognize it. This is not about becoming some sort of Zen sage, never angered, never off-balance. Of course, you will be angry. In many situations you <u>should</u> be angry. It may even keep you alive. The problem is when anger justifies anything from treating aggravating or troublesome people with contempt to actions that are either immoral or illegal on the extreme edge.

Figure 35 Protecting Your Family From What You Otherwise Would Bring Home

Another type of righteous anger is that evoked when someone does something so upsetting that one feels annihilation of the perpetrator is the only justifiable response. For example, in the course of my professional responsibilities, I have had to be in the presence of the perpetrators of child abuse or sexual assault. Having done my job well, so that, for example, I get a confession, evidence to make a case, or ensure that the abusive individual never has access to their victim again, I, nonetheless have left the room feeling a failure because I did not take his throat between my hands and squeeze the life out of him for what he did.

I've made sure that I never brought this feeling home. I sit in my car or maybe going to a quiet place in the house or yard, and in particular, and enact Circular Breathing, the method described in the next chapter, so that when I walked into the presence of my wife and children, the only thing I ever bring home is me. Nobody uninvited will walk into the house with me—otherwise, how can I claim to be protecting my family?

CHAPTER 36

Circular Breathing—
Be The Eye In The Center
Of The Hurricane

Aggression and violence can smash through a previously peaceful day with the suddenness and force of a hurricane. Aggression does not only take over the day; it may take you over too. However, when you can respond by stepping coolly into the worst of situations, all the chaos begins to revolve around you. When you control yourself, you control the chaos as well. The root of this skill lies in breath control. Using a method called 'circular breathing,' where you breathe slowly, with focused attention, you regain control of your physical self. When you control your body, you control your life. Then you are in a position to take control of the crisis as well as the person causing it.

Two Variations

Circular breathing is derived from East Asian martial traditions and was used to keep warriors calm on the battlefield. There are two variations. Try both, alternating between them, until you know which one works best for you. From that point on, exclusively practice the one you prefer. *If you train regularly, it will kick in automatically, rather than being something you must think about.*

Circular Breathing Method #1: Down the Front, Up the Back

- Sit comfortably, feet on the floor, hands in your lap. (This is the posture that you first practice. Once you are skilled in this technique, you can be in any position whatsoever.)

- Sit relaxed, but upright. Do not slump or twist your posture.

- Keep your eyes open. (<u>As you practice, so you will do.</u> If you practice with your eyes closed, your newly trained nervous system will send an impulse to close your eyes in emergency situations. If you want to use a breathing method for relaxation or to get *away* from your problems, use another method altogether.)

- Breathe in through the nose.

- Imagine the air traveling in a line down the front of your body to a point 2 inches below the navel.

- Momentarily pause, letting the breath remain in a dynamic equilibrium.

- As you exhale, imagine the air looping around your lower body, between your legs and up through the base of your spine.

- Continue to exhale, imagining the air going up your spine and around your head and then out of your nose.

Circular Breathing Method #2: Down the Back, Up the Front

- Sit comfortably, feet on the floor, hands in your lap. (This is the posture that you first practice. Once you are skilled in this technique, you can be in any position whatsoever.)

- Sit relaxed, but upright. Do not slump or twist your posture.

- Keep your eyes open. (<u>As you practice, so you will do.</u> If you practice with your eyes closed, your newly trained nervous system will send an impulse to close your eyes in emergency situations. If you want to use a breathing method for relaxation or to get *away* from your problems, use another method altogether.)

- Breathe in through the nose.

- Imagine the air going up around your head, looping down the back, falling down each vertebra, continuing down past the base of the spine to the perineum, and looping again, this time up the front of the body to a point 2 inches below the navel.

- Momentarily pause, letting the breath remain in a dynamic equilibrium.

- As you exhale, imagining the air ascending up the centerline of your body and out your nose.

How To Practice Circular Breathing

Some people find that imagining their breath has light or color is helpful. Others take a finger or object to trace a line down and around the centerline of the body to help focus their attention. Again, choose which works best for you.

When you first practice, do so while seated and balanced. Once you develop some skill, try circular breathing standing, leaning, or even while driving. Most people find that after a short period of time they do not need to visualize the circulation of the breath. You literally will feel it, a ring of energy running through your body. You begin to feel balanced and ready for anything.

Once you are comfortable with your chosen pattern of breathing, experiment with it in slightly stressful circumstances, like being caught in traffic, dealing with an upset family member, or sitting through a meeting as a supervisor drones on about new paperwork requirements. When you can better manage yourself in these slightly aggravating or anxiety-provoking situations, you will automatically shift into this mode of breathing when a crisis hits. There will no longer be a need to tell yourself to 'do' circular breathing. It will become reflexive, automatic, replacing old patterns of breathing that actually increased anxiety or anger within you.

When Should You Use Circular Breathing?

The way you organize physically affects your thinking. For example, if you assume the posture and breathing of a depressed person (slumped body, shallow breathing, sighing), and maintain it awhile, you will actually start to feel depressed. Similarly, if you clench your fists, and start glaring around you with a lot of tension in your body, you will start to feel angry. (You have probably observed people working themselves up from anger to rage in this manner.) Similarly, circular breathing creates its own mindset: one adaptable and ready for anything, equally prepared for an easy conversation and for a fight, yet fixed on neither.

This method of breathing is very helpful when you are anticipating a potentially dangerous situation, anything from walking down a hallway to check out loud voices from an office to seeing potential danger in the parking lot as you are walking to your car. This breathing activates the entire nervous system in a way that enhances both creativity and the ability to survive.

Even in the middle of a confrontation, particularly a verbal one, there are many times when this breathing will have a very powerful effect. Not only do we get more stressed or upset in the presence of an upset person, but we also become more peaceful in the presence of a calm one. People tend to template their mood to the most powerful individual close by. You surely know people who, when they walk onto a scene, often calm it down before they have said a word. You have probably seen the opposite as well, where a certain person appears and it immediately gets worse. Using this breathing method is a vital tool in making you the former type, a man or woman of quiet power.

Use this method of breathing after the crisis as well. You will need to regroup to go on with the rest of your day. Circular breathing will bring you back to a calm and relaxed state, prepared to handle the next crisis, should one occur.

Figure 36   Seeing close and far at the same time – Breathing is the Most Important Thing of All

A law enforcement officer has described to me using this breathing on a daily basis. She states that in an adrenalized state, she tends to get tunnel vision—she is great at picking up danger 'inside the tunnel,' but she has found herself literally blind to things outside that hyper-focused area. Using 'circular' breathing, she finds that she is still aware of how the angry person in front of her is shifting his stance, where his hands are, and if he is trying to move close to her or achieve an advantageous angle of attack. At the same time, however, she is able to perceive what is happening to the side, and even across the street, or in a window above ground level. Moreover, her hearing and other senses are enhanced.

Not only does this enable her to pick up potential danger coming from other sources, she is also better able to perceive what is NOT dangerous. Finally, her relaxed centered breathing has no 'fight within it,' but she is best prepared to fight. People naturally calm down with her because she is calm.

Of course, I hope that you, my reader, are able to learn every skill in this book. But if you can only learn one, this is it. If you properly organize your breathing, your body self-organizes as well. And when the mind perceives its own body centered and relaxed, it bases its own responses—cognitions and emotions—with the FACT that the body is relaxed and in control. The right words come to you and the right actions follow.

Appendices

APPENDIX I

Managing Threats
To Your Family

By threatening your family, aggressive individuals can create within you a sense of helplessness and desperation. The threat is usually empty, made in the heat of the moment or with the intention of terrifying you and yours. You must, however, take any such threats seriously, because it is almost impossible to know when the threat is real or not. And, truth be told, a bit of preventative planning and education of your family members as to their need to be aware is never a bad thing. The development of a family safety plan is not enough; review your plan regularly with your family. You should do the following:

- Inform your family of any threats and of the need to take protective action. In regard to children, your responsibility is to explain <u>everything they *need* to know, but no more.</u> Furthermore, if you display your own fears excessively, you will only frighten your family members. To this end, I strongly recommend that you acquire two books by Gavin de Becker: *The Gift of Fear* and *Protecting the Gift.*[6]

- **Inform local law enforcement.** Police professionals will assist you in drawing up a safety plan as well as considering what, if any, action they can take on your behalf.

- **Review home security.** Are you a soft target or a hard target? A soft target is easily accessible, predictable, and unaware of danger.

---

6   See: de Becker, G. (1997). *The Gift of Fear: Survival signals that protect us from violence.* U.S. and Canada: Little Brown; and (1999). *Protecting the gift: Keeping children and teenagers safe (and parents sane)* New York: Random House, New York.

A hard target is not easily accessible, or predictable. Adequate lighting and the use of quality locks, doors, and windows will limit the ability of an intruder to enter your home. Consult with your local police department as to how to make your home more secure. Some departments will be more willing than others to send a professional out to walk through and around your home to inform you of security gaps. There are also excellent books on home security available. Consider a home alarm system.

- **Firearms.** If you choose to acquire a firearm, every member of your family *must* attend a firearm safety and instruction course, and firearms should be stored and cared for accordingly.

- **Dogs.** In some ways, dogs are a better security option than a firearm. Unlike humans, a well-trained dog, particularly certain breeds, will not hesitate to act when they perceive a threat. Dogs will also provide you with an early warning system, detecting sounds and smells that you cannot. Further discussion of dog breeds and training is well beyond the scope of this book, but dogs can be one of the most important aspects of home security.

- **Scan your surroundings.** Your family members must learn to scan their surroundings and note anything out of the ordinary. Remind family to report suspicious people and cars.

- **Inform employers and schools**. Do this so they are aware of the identity of the potential assailant. Make clear to school officials exactly who is allowed to meet or pick-up your children.

- **Change your routine.** As much as possible, travel by different routes and at different times. Be unpredictable.

- **Safety in numbers.** Neither you nor your family members should be the last person to leave the workplace or school. Enlist co-coworkers, coaches, teachers, etc., to be part of a team.

- **Notification of travel plans.** Notify your office and family of travel plans, and ask that they not reveal any travel plans or other schedules.

- **Be careful about giving out personal information.** This can be difficult with children, as they happily exchange information with their friends or others. Remind them to be careful of strangers, and to report any such inquiries. Do not forget about social networking sites such as Facebook and Instagram, and other dangers of the Internet. (Do some research—what you think is popular is probably out of date. Your child may be agreeable to not putting information on a social media site that he or she hardly uses—it is the one you do not know about that may be the problem).

- **Plan an escape route.** Figure out the best ways to escape from the home and rehearse this with family members. You can combine this with fire drills, something the children are already familiar with from school.

- **A safe haven.** Arrange with trustworthy neighbors to a) watch the neighborhood for the person(s) of concern near your house b) a safe haven for your family to go if your home—or they—are under attack.

- **Plan how to ask for help.** Plan how to ask for help if in public and how best to call for help if needed. If your children are alone and there are no nearby police cars, the best stranger to ask for help is a *woman*, as women are far less likely to be a threat. Of course, this is not the case if a woman is the threatening individual.

- **Code words.** Teach your children a code word or challenge that must be answered by strange individuals. This includes neighbors, and in some cases, relatives. For example, a person approaches your child after school and says, "Tasha, your mother and father were injured in an automobile accident. The police told me to take you to the hospital! Please come with me now." Your child should have been taught to keep his/her distance, looking for escape routes as she asks, "What's the word?" If the person does not reply immediately the child should run to a safe haven and describe the individual as best they can.

- **Post emergency numbers near each telephone extension.**
  Establish safe havens to escape to in times of danger. If possible, enlist your neighbors in your safety plan.

Appendix I Glad to Meet You—It May Save My Life

We live lives alone, in close proximity. Many of us do not know the names of our neighbors. We do not say hello to them—often, there is no opportunity as people hop in their cars, drive away from their homes and go about their lives elsewhere. Rather than sitting on the porch in the evening, catching up on our children's lives, we use social media in a pale imitation of community.

For many of us who live in urban environments, it is even worse. There is no area in the street to pass the time, and we ride together on elevators to our apartments, staring straight ahead or gazing intently at our smart phones.

If no one knows you, will anyone open the door if you are desperately knocking, seeking help?

Therefore, to truly plan to protect your family, get to know your neighbors (you'll also possibly learn whom *not* to trust). Furthermore, for those in an urban environment, drop by the local stores, and not only buy something, even small items, but engage the people in the shop in conversation. Imagine, sometime in the future then, your children are coming home from school when they realize that they're being followed. They step into the local store, be it café or bodega, and tell the clerk, whom they know, the one who has been kind and trustworthy already, that they need help. That adult is more willing to protect them because we humans are more likely to protect those we know—our own tribe, so to speak.

APPENDIX II

What About
Where I Work?

No matter how skilled you may become at verbal de-escalation, you will sometimes have to deal with belligerent individuals at your worksite who may be unable, or more likely, unwilling to stop themselves from acting aggressively, no matter what you might say or do. Whenever possible, you should enlist the help of others rather than trying to solve such dangerous situations on your own.

However, it is not enough to be *willing* to help. Everyone must know *how* to help. You cannot create an effective safety plan on the spot. When things do go wrong, you must know what to do—together. When you are focused as an individual *and* coordinated as a team, you will be far more effective in managing the aggressive person.

Places that have a well-coordinated and well-practiced safety plan feel different as well because potential aggressors:
- See fewer opportunities to attack.
- Find fewer pretexts to justify an attack.
- See little chance of success in carrying out an attack.

Physical Site Safety
Your workplace is an extension of yourself, and although you should be comfortable, safety should not be sacrificed for convenience. You enhance the security of everyone when the design of your worksite takes into account the possibility that aggressive people may try to act out.

In general, your personal office should have a minimum of furniture and clutter. Establishing a truly safe workplace environment may be difficult due to limitations in architectural design, as well as the financial constraints of your business. However, there are many inexpensive ways of enhancing security, requiring only that you and your co-workers be alert to safety issues and communicate with one another. Some or all of these examples may apply to where you work:

- Control ingress and egress to the office itself. Particularly in worksites where many people arrive every day, a secure reception area should be established to control the flow of individuals. Ideally, the door leading from the reception area into the office itself should remain locked at all times. Someone, either an employee, or in high-security facilities, a Security Professional should escort each individual into and out of the office. Do not allow people to wander unescorted through your worksite.

- Security doors must remain locked if they are to be effective. Propping a security door open, or leaving the door unlocked, defeats its intended purpose.

- Particularly in larger agencies, specific rooms should be established and used to conduct interviews. Such rooms can remain free from any extraneous office equipment, leaving the room free of many potential weapons.

- If you meet potentially hostile individuals in your own work space:
  - Pens, pencils, staplers, paper punches, and other office equipment can be used as weapons. Keep your desks clear—you can always have them near at hand in a desk drawer.
  - Are picture frames or corkboards secured to the walls? Any item that can be removed from the walls or picked up easily is a potential weapon. *NOTE: I was once knocked out by a wooden frame 'Frisbeed' between my eyes at close range.*
  - Loose chair parts and light furniture can be used as weapons as well. Make sure that all necessary office furniture

and equipment are in good condition and in proper working order. When designing an office, or acquiring new furniture, safety must be considered in addition to comfort and aesthetics.

- Personal photographs of family members and loved ones should not be able to be viewed by strangers or others who may be hostile—with current cell-phone technology, they can be imaged and used inappropriately. Not only will they attract the interest of the predatory individual, such photographs may exacerbate the envy of the 'failure in life' who, seeing the picture of your good fortune, wonders why you get to be so 'lucky' when they are not.

- Outside your personal office space, give consideration to all hallways, stairwells, staff and public elevators, parking and storage areas, and the reception area. Are there adequate sight lines to see who is entering the reception area? Is the lighting adequate in hallways, stairwells, and parking areas?

Communication for Emergencies

- **Develop an emergency communication plan.** Emergency numbers, as required by your profession and also based on who may appear on your worksite, should be programmed into the office phone system or posted near each telephone in the security office. Beyond 9-1-1, this can include poison control, child or elder adult protective services, or the mental health professionals who, in your state or province, are responsible for placing severely mentally ill people in a hospital.

- **Whenever possible, use a land line to call for emergency assistance.** Your address will automatically be available to emergency call takers, letting them know your location even when you cannot speak freely. If you use a cell phone to call for help, the FIRST thing you should say is your physical location, i.e., "I am in Building 4, seventh floor of the Lander Company.

195

407 Collison St, Glendale. There is a very angry man, wearing a Chicago Blackhawk jersey, threatening our office manager. We are on lock-down, etc."

- **Emergency Call Buttons.** Some agencies install emergency call buttons that trigger an audible or silent alarm. Some even include lights over the doorways of rooms that illuminate, designating where the crisis is occurring. Other companies offer 'key fob' type panic alarms, which are portable and can be kept on the person. However, installing such buttons is not enough. Your agency should have regular drills to be sure that they actually work, and that the designated people actually respond when an emergency button is pressed.

- **Code Phrase** Because you may find yourself in a situation where you need to summon help without alerting the hostile individual, your office or company should develop emergency code words, names or phrases that will activate emergency procedures, summon help and trigger a call to law enforcement. This code phrase can be used over the public address system to summon aid, as well as over your office phone, or in conversation with a co-worker. A code word should be selected that can be placed in context to the situation being discussed without arousing suspicion. There must be consistent training in using code words or phrases so that staffs' reaction to them will be as immediate as it would be were they to hear a siren. Attrition of staff requires both updating those on your current roster and training new hires.

Appendix II Figure 1 Code Words

Whenever the agreed-upon code word or phrase is voiced, no matter what the **apparent** context of the call, the recipient knows that the designated safety response plan must be initiated.

For example:

- "I'm in the 2nd conference room. Would **Mr. HOLMES** get me our information on hiring practices concerning those under the age of twenty-one" In this case, the use of the name **HOLMES,** by prearrangement means, "I need help right now."
- "I need an immediate consult with **Mr._HOLMES** concerning whether we are required to call the union as soon as a report of possible theft is filed."
- "Could **Mr._HOLMES** please come here with the records I was talking about? I'm in conference room B."
- (Over the PA system) Calling **MR. HOLMES** to the lobby of building four.

- **Secondary Code Phrase.** Some agencies use a second code to simply call one person down to check out the situation or offer support. Rather than using a fictitious name in this circumstance, I recommend a **code word** that is somewhat unusual: to alert the person that the situation is heated and it may be necessary that they stand by, ready to assist. In this circumstance, you do not have an emergency yet. There is, therefore, no need to obscure your intentions from the person. Instead, you could call the front desk or a supervisor and say, for example, "Mr. DeVore is troubled by our recent phone call to his insurance company. Would you send Ms. Bargetta to this office to **lend a hand** in explaining things to him." In this case, the somewhat stilted 'lend a hand' is used, rather than the more common 'help,' and this word is designated, agency-wide, as the code that the situation demands immediate attention.

Appendix II   Figure 2 Explicit Announcements in Emergencies

There are other situations in which you must inform everyone in your facility, without ambiguity, that they are in an emergency situation. In these cases, speak explicitly. For example: "A man with a gun, wearing a red jacket and brown pants is in the building. He was last seen on the second floor. Staff must initiate emergency procedures now!"

With proper planning and attention to detail, many potential emergencies can be curtailed before they develop into a harmful situation. Of course, even the best-laid plans will not prevent an emergency from arising, which is why regular practice of the safety plan is a requirement for the safety of all concerned. Regular practice will also highlight areas of the response plan that need to be modified and improved upon, *before* a true emergency occurs. Staff who have developed a safety mindset will foster a safer and more supportive office culture, one where safety is paramount.

The Five Ws: WHAT Kind Of Information Do You Need When An Emergency Is Happening?

There is some information that is absolutely required when trying to assess threat level in any emergency. Therefore, the reporter of any crisis should find out:

- **Where?** Get the location of where the incident is happening, and get the informant to tell you again! Absolutely nothing can be accomplished if emergency responders cannot reach the correct scene.

- **What?** Always ensure that you know what is going on, and do not assume that the first thing the person tells you is the real story! Information tends to vary as the level of stress or urgency increases. Descriptions of people, activities, weapons, and the type of violence may be inconsistent, leading responders to a conclusion not necessarily accurate. It is important to listen to information being presented, at the same time understanding the circumstances under which it is being presented.

- **Who?** Be sure to find out everyone who is involved: those presenting a threat, those who are injured or victims, and others on the scene. As obvious and basic a statement as this may be, the irrational or confusing verbiage of frightened or agitated individuals can cause the person taking information to miss essential data.

- **When?** When did the crisis happen: recently, currently, or is it about to happen? How urgent a situation is it NOW?

- **Weapons.** We must do everything necessary and possible to keep our police officers, firefighters, and EMTs safe. Questions about weapons and their locations, a history of violence, past or current threats to responders, drug or alcohol use, and any other potential dangers must be answered as fully as humanly possible.

Staying Calm By Being Prepared For The Worst

Do not shut your eyes to signs of danger. The calm of a trained person is very different from the calm of the clueless person. You must be conscious of what the aggressor is doing and the likely meaning and implications of that. While you are trying to calm or soothe them, or while you are controlling the crisis, remain conscious of the following:

- Where are your escape routes? Is something blocking your way out?

- Are there any obstacles, sharp corners or other hazards that you need to avoid?
- Are there any weapons around that can be used against you, or that you can pick up in your own defense? Do you have access to whatever weapon you are bearing?
- Is the person's aggressiveness escalating?
- Do they have allies, confederates who are waiting for you to get off-guard, at which point they will join in the attack?
- What are your non-verbal behaviors? Are you getting mad too? If so, it is best to disengage or you will merely get very angry together and the situation could become explosive.
- Where is your 'team?' Is other staff organizing to help you?

Similar to our previous discussions, the 'drama' of considering an attack within your worksite can obscure the fact that you already know how to plan in the midst of action. Consider these examples:

- You come to a four-way intersection or a round-about and while driving, must calculate who has the right of way, who (if any) are violating the right of way, are there pedestrians crossing the street or emerging from a shadowy area?
- You have to usher your three children through a crowd during a street festival or celebration. They could easily get lost, and you do not want to bump into anyone or drop your packages.
- You are preparing a dinner for guests, while supervising your children's homework, while keeping your one ill child in bed, and mentally preparing for a presentation at work due on Monday.

Of course, the missing component in these examples is fear. It's much easier to multi-task when you are not even thinking of survival. However, detailed, logical, repetitive preparation for emergencies means that in such a rare event, you find yourself on familiar ground—you have already imposed upon yourself a pattern of behavior so that you respond without thought, even amidst your fear.

Calling the Police

Police should be called when anyone is at physical risk or when an aggressive individual is so disruptive that their behavior cannot be modulated. It is your responsibility to give as complete information as possible, including a description of the aggressor, their current location, whether they have weapons, and their current behavior and potential risk. Whenever possible, inform emergency responders of exactly what help you are requesting. You must understand that the police, as emergency responders in cases of potential danger, will take over to establish safety based on *their* assessment of risk at that moment.

Appendix II Figure 3

My wife had trained in a martial art for about nine months. Among the practices at the school she attended, a judo and aikido dojo, was methods of safely taking a fall. They would practice this, tens, even hundreds of times in a single evening. Among the techniques is a 'front fall,' where, falling forward, one drops into the plank position: forearms and the balls of the feet are all that touch the ground.

One evening, seven months pregnant, she was going down a hill on a bicycle very fast, and the front brake caliper broke and jammed the wheel. The bike stopped dead and flipped forward. She flew over the handle bars and landed in a plank position, belly not touching the concrete, landing with such perfect force distribution that she didn't even have a bruise or abraded skin.

Because of the frequent repetitions, in a life-threatening emergency, her situation in time and space was familiar and she landed perfectly.

ABOUT THE AUTHOR

Ellis Amdur

Edgework founder Ellis Amdur received his B.A. in psychology from Yale University in 1974 and his M.A. in psychology from Seattle University in 1990. He is both a National Certified Counselor and a State Certified Child Mental Health Specialist.

Amdur has trained in various martial arts systems since the late 1960's, spending thirteen of these years studying in Japan. He is a recognized expert in classical and modern Japanese martial traditions and has authored three iconoclastic books on the subject, as well as one instructional DVD.

Since his return to America in 1988, Ellis Amdur has worked in the field of crisis intervention. He has developed a range of training and consultation services, as well as a unique style of assessment and psychotherapy. All are based on a combination of phenomenological psychology and the underlying philosophical premises of classical Japanese martial traditions. Amdur's professional philosophy can best be summed up in this idea: the development of a person's integrity and dignity is the paramount virtue. This can only occur when people live courageously, regardless of the circumstances, and take responsibility for their roles in making the changes they desire. He has authored and co-authored a number of specialized books on the de-escalation of aggression, like this one, but going into far more detail that is specific to those in various professions. Please refer to www.edgeworkbooks.com for a complete description of each of his books.

Ellis Amdur is a dynamic public speaker and trainer who presents his work throughout the United States and internationally. He is noted for his sometimes outrageous humor as well as his profound breadth of knowledge. His vivid descriptions of aggressive and mentally ill people and his true-to-life role-playing of the behaviors in question give participants an almost first-hand experience of facing the real individuals in question. Please see Amdur's website: www.edgework.info for further information

Made in United States
North Haven, CT
20 October 2023

42992292R00124